Four Horsemen, Four Hearts

Responding to the Gospel in Revelation 6

By

Paul Haynes

with Curtis Rittenour

TEACH Services, Inc.
PUBLISHING
www.TEACHServices.com • (800) 367-1844

World rights reserved. This book or any portion thereof may not be copied or reproduced in any form or manner whatever, except as provided by law, without the written permission of the publisher, except by a reviewer who may quote brief passages in a review.

This book was written to provide truthful information in regard to the subject matter covered. The author assumes full responsibility for the accuracy of all facts and quotations as cited in this book. The opinions expressed in this book are the author's personal views and interpretation of the Bible, Spirit of Prophecy, and/or contemporary authors and do not necessarily reflect those of TEACH Services, Inc.

This book is sold with the understanding that the publisher is not engaged in giving spiritual, legal, medical, or other professional advice. If authoritative advice is needed, the reader should seek the counsel of a competent professional.

All Scripture quotations, unless otherwise noted, are from the *New King James Version.*

Front Cover Photograph by Oleg Senkov/Bigstock.com
Back Cover Illustration by Jill E. Judge

Copyright © 2013 TEACH Services, Inc.
ISBN-13: 978-1-4796-0059-5 (Paperback)
ISBN-13: 978-1-4796-0060-1 (epub)
ISBN-13: 978-1-4796-0061-8 (Kindle/Mobi)
Library of Congress Control Number: 2013933030

Published by

www.TEACHServices.com • (800) 367-1844

Table of Contents

Foreword v

Introduction vii

Chapter 1   Four Horses and Four Riders 12

Chapter 2   Heaven's Throne Room 18

Chapter 3   Another View of the Heavenly Sanctuary 31

Chapter 4   Creatures Around God's
                   Throne and a Book Unsealed 48

Chapter 5   The Message of the White Horse:
                   The Gospel Received? 64

Chapter 6   The Message of the Red Horse:
                   Peace or Fear? 77

Chapter 7   The Message of the Black Horse:
                   Freedom or Slavery? 87

Chapter 8   The Message of the Green Horse:
                   Life or Death? 96

Chapter 9	Four Soils, Four Responses	112
Chapter 10	Parallel Pictures: Seeds and Horses	121
Chapter 11	How Will You Respond?	127

FOREWORD

A Personal Experience

When I arrived at the hospital where I was working, I walked into the building with my coat in one hand while dragging my computer and books on a luggage cart with the other. Making my way down the hall toward the room where I would be staying for the next few days, my mind was somewhere else. I was still back home, sitting at my desk, studying a passage in Revelation 6.

God, why would You give John a vision about four horses? What is the relation of the horses to Your throne? Why would You have one horse with a positive message and three horses with a negative one? Lord, I do not understand. It does not make sense. Please help me to comprehend this vision.

When I reached the room where I was staying and began to put the key into the door, I suddenly had a strong impression: *Study the Parable of the Sower.* I was surprised and thought: *What does the Parable of the Sower have to do with the four horsemen of Revelation 6?*

This experience happened six years ago. Like opening a door, the Holy Spirit has opened my mind to see in God's Word many parallels. I have learned that one part of Scripture opens the door to another. Could it be that the book of Revelation has diamonds of truth waiting in "rooms" yet to be opened by comparing Scriptures? The book of Revelation was not given to fascinate the reader with prophecies of the future. Nor was it meant to simply grab the reader's attention by speaking of a dragon and beasts, of a lion and lamb. Revelation is about salvation—*your* salvation. Through my many years of studying this book, I have discovered a deeper purpose in John's visions. It began when I asked myself: *What is God saying to me?* I had spent much time asking what God was trying to tell John, which was an important step. However, when I began to sincerely ask: *Lord, what message do you have for me in this book?* I saw prophecy in a new light.

Perhaps you are also standing in front of your own door asking questions of God. Have you ever inquired: *What does the book of Revelation have to do with my life? What does the future hold for me? How do these strange symbols, such as the four horsemen of Revelation 6, affect my life?* John's account in Revelation 4–6 is often relegated to the past, yet it is a key that opens a door of truth for our time. It tells of God's plan to save our world and eradicate evil. It contains a message to "come and see" as well as to *go and tell*. The essence of John's vision of the throne room of Revelation 4 and 5 is Christ's ministry on behalf of fallen humanity. The message of the four horsemen of Revelation 6 is about taking the gospel to the world. Christ's work and our response are the focus of this book. The consequences of our response will be eternal. Will you join me in opening the door to receive God's urgent warning portrayed by horses and riders?

Introduction

The "four horsemen of the Apocalypse" is a term used in popular culture to represent a variety of things. It is also the nickname of four players on a college football team. Comic book characters have been named after them. It has been the basis of movie plots and novels. Video games capitalize on the phrase. A book on marriage even uses the idea to describe the four most destructive behaviors hurting relationships. Almost all references to the four horsemen depict them as something evil. Most often, they bring doom and gloom. They seem to be characters from whom we should run. One interpretation even depicts the rider of the white horse as the antichrist. Most people have never even read Revelation 6, where the term originated, let alone the rest of the book.

Revealing Christ

Can we know the meaning of these horsemen? Are they good or are they evil? Do they represent Christ and His good angels or Satan and his evil angels? To guide us in our search for answers, we need to start at the beginning of the book and ask: *What is John's basic purpose in writing?* Revelation begins with a clear message—"The Revelation of Jesus Christ, which God gave Him to show His servants—things which must shortly take place" (Rev. 1:1). Revelation is a Christ-centered book with a relevant message that God meant for us to share. Its focus is Jesus and His work in heaven for the salvation of the world. We will learn as we study that Revelation was not only for Christians in John's day but is even more relevant for Christians today.

The writer, John, is a prisoner "for the word of God and for the testimony of Jesus Christ" on the island of Patmos (Rev. 1:9). John was banished for sharing the gospel and giving the "testimony of Jesus," which is a prophetic testimony. In the opening verses, he tells how this message came to him. "And He [Jesus] sent and signified *it* by His angel to His servant John, who bore witness to the word of God, and to the testimony of Jesus Christ, to all things that he saw" (Rev. 1:1, 2). Here we find a chain of communication between God and man, which we will learn more about later.

You might feel intimidated studying prophetic literature that is full of mysterious symbols and strange beasts. Yet, it should encourage you to know that God has promised to bless those who study this remarkable book. "Blessed is he who reads and those who hear the words of this prophecy, and keep those things which are written in it; for the time is near" (Rev. 1:3). What are His blessings? First, God blesses us when we read Revelation. Next, God blesses those who hear these words. Finally, God blesses those who "keep those things which are written in it." When we are obedient to the message of Revelation, we become like John, who "bore witness" and delivered God's warning message to the world.

Light for Today

Is Revelation relevant for our time? The King James Version translates the end of verse 3: "the time is at hand." The New King James Version translates it: "the time is near." The Amplified New Testament expands the phrase to say: "for the time [for them to be fulfilled] is near." Verse 1 tells us that these things "must shortly take place" (NKJV). Was John referring to events that would occur in his time, two thousand years ago, or was he rather referring to events that would occur at a later time and in our age? Ellen White shares this insight:

The prophets of God spoke less for their own time than for the ages to come, and especially for the generation that would live amid the last scenes of this earth's history.... (*Signs of the Times*, January 13, 1898)

The generation described would be the *last* generation to stand on the earth before the second coming of Jesus Christ. Who is that last generation? Are we the last generation, or is another to follow us? Leslie Hardinge comments: "Now that we are in 'the time of the end' the prophetic light from Daniel and other Old Testament seers has become present light" (Leslie Hardinge, *Jesus is My Judge: Meditations on the Book of Daniel*, pp. 229, 230).

The book of Daniel, the other major apocalyptic book in Scripture, also speaks of "the time of the end." Daniel puzzled over the visions given him by God and wondered when the events predicted would take place. A brief look at the phrase "the time of the end" in Daniel opens our understanding to its meaning in Revelation.

Daniel 12 begins with Christ, our heavenly High Priest, completing His work in the sanctuary. The chapter is a prophecy about the end of time on this earth. Listen to the angel's comment to Daniel after Daniel received the vision: "'But you, Daniel, shut up the words, and seal the book until the time of the end ...'" (Dan. 12:4). As he was thinking about this command, Daniel was given another vision. Once more, he wants to know "what *shall be* the end of these *things*?" (Dan. 12:8). The angel answers, "Go *your way*, Daniel, for the words *are* closed up and sealed till the time of the end" (Dan. 12:9).

Ellen White addresses how and when Daniel's book would be unsealed. She writes: "The things revealed to Daniel were afterward complemented by the revelation made to John on the Isle of Patmos" (*Testimonies to Ministers*, p. 114). She then describes which message marked its opening:

> Daniel stood in his lot to bear his testimony which was sealed until the time of the end, when the first angel's message should be proclaimed to our world … The book of Daniel is unsealed in the revelation to John, and carries us forward to the last scenes of this earth's history. (*Testimonies to Ministers*, p. 115)

Christ unsealed the book of Daniel through the revelation to John of the message that would be proclaimed during in the time of the end. That message is the three angels' messages. Thus, the proclamation of the first angel's message marked its beginning. When did the first angel's message first go out?

> Shortly after the fulfilment of some of the signs that the Saviour foretold would be seen before his second coming, there took place throughout the Christian world a great religious awakening. Students of prophecy came to the conclusion that the time of the end was at hand. In the book of Daniel they read: "Unto two thousand and three hundred days, then shall the sanctuary be cleansed." … Searching the Scriptures for further light, and comparing this prophetic period with the records of historians, they learned that the twenty-three hundred days extended to the year 1844. (*Southern Watchman*, January 24, 1905)

The time of the end began when the 2,300-day prophecy expired and "the first angel's message was proclaimed to our world." Thus, the time of the end began in the year 1844. We are living in that time. Revelation tells us "what should be in these last days." It does not give the exact date of the close of "the time of the end," but it tells of events that will occur just before it happens.

A common interpretation of the four horsemen of Revelation 6 is that they represent aspects of the political history of the church. That is certainly a valid historicist application. However, the messages to the seven churches each end with a statement that implies that Revelation has a spiritual application for all time, including ours: "He who has an ear, let him hear what the Spirit says to the churches."

If we are indeed living in the final days of earth's history, then the message of Revelation is urgent. It was written to prepare us for events soon to happen. As with the other books of the Bible, we need the Holy Spirit to open our understanding regarding this book. This message of salvation, also spoken of in Revelation 14 as the three angels' messages, is the only hope for our dying world. Our love for others should compel us to share God's message of preparation and warning with people that we encounter each day. How will Revelation's four horses help us accomplish this?

Chapter 1

Four Horses and Four Riders

Have you ever been in a hurry to share an important message with someone? Perhaps you have even been in a life or death situation in which a 911 phone call was employed to save someone's life. Paul Revere would surely know how you feel. He represents the classic example in United States history of the proclamation of an urgent message. Mr. Revere rode a fast horse from town to town shouting his message while galloping through the villages. Do you remember reading or hearing this famous poem in grade school?

> Listen, my children, and you shall hear
> Of the midnight ride of Paul Revere,
> On the eighteenth of April, in Seventy-five;
> Hardly a man is now alive
> Who remembers that famous day and year.
>
> He said to his friend, "If the British march
> By land or sea from the town to-night,
> Hang a lantern aloft in the belfry arch
> Of the North Church tower as a signal light,—
> One if by land, and two if by sea;
> And I on the opposite shore will be,
> Ready to ride and spread the alarm

> Through every Middlesex village and farm,
> For the country folk to be up and to arm."

Revere was joined in his ride by William Dawes and about forty other riders, yet, because of Longfellow's poem, it is Paul Revere whom we remember for the midnight ride. Traversing the region on horseback and waking his neighbors from their sleep, he proclaimed: *Get up, get ready, and get armed. The enemy is approaching.* The country folk certainly heard, saw, and responded as the Revolutionary War began. The rest is history. Revelation 6 speaks of four horses and four riders. Do they have a similar message?

"Come and See."

Revelation 6 begins with an invitation. "Now I saw when the Lamb opened one of the seals; and I heard one of the four living creatures saying with a voice like thunder, 'Come and see'" (Rev. 6:1). Who is the Lamb? What do the seals represent? Who are the four living creatures? Before we discuss these details, let us simply read through to verse 8 for a quick overview of the passage.

> And I looked, and behold, a white horse. He who sat on it had a bow; and a crown was given to him, and he went out conquering and to conquer. When He opened the second seal, I heard the second living creature saying, "Come and see." Another horse, fiery red, went out. And it was granted to the one who sat on it to take peace from the earth, and that people should kill one another; and there was given to him a great sword. When He opened the third seal, I heard the third living creature say, "Come and see." So I looked, and behold, a black horse, and he who sat on it had a pair of scales in his hand.

And I heard a voice in the midst of the four living creatures saying, "A quart of wheat for a denarius, and three quarts of barley for a denarius; and do not harm the oil and the wine." When He opened the fourth seal, I heard the voice of the fourth living creature saying, "Come and see." So I looked, and behold, a pale horse. And the name of him who sat on it was Death, and Hades followed with him. And power was given to them over a fourth of the earth, to kill with sword, with hunger, with death, and by the beasts of the earth. (Rev. 6:2–8)

What do we see in this passage? There are four horses and four riders. Each horse has a different color. There are other interesting details. The riders are briefly described. Sometimes the passage tells us what they wear, and other times it tells what they are holding in their hands. Once a voice is heard from among the four living creatures. Yet, all of them bear a cryptic message as they go out. What reason would there be for using horses in this passage?

The Horse as a Symbol

What is so special about horses? Horses are built with strength. They have a well-developed sense of balance and a strong fight-or-flight instinct. They can run quickly from predators. Horses even have the ability to sleep standing up or lying down. Yet, horses are not all alike. The 300 or so breeds of horses that exist today can be loosely divided into three categories. Hot bloods are spirited horses that have speed and endurance. Cold bloods are slower horses, like draft horses, that can do heavy work. Warm bloods are crosses between hot and cold bloods and were bred for specific riding purposes.

Horses were often used throughout history in warfare. The first use of horses in battle is found in the Ancient Near East around 3000 BC. One of the earliest horse training manuals was written in Greece about 1350 BC and explains how to use horses in war. In the Orient, light hot-blooded horses were used in war because of their speed and endurance. Because they were smaller in size, the rider carried lightweight tack and few weapons.

The Bible uses the horse as a symbol. Notice God's description of the horse to Job.

> Have you given the horse strength? Have you clothed his neck with thunder? Can you frighten him like a locust? His majestic snorting strikes terror. He paws in the valley, and rejoices in his strength; he gallops into the clash of arms. He mocks at fear, and is not frightened; nor does he turn back from the sword. (Job 39:19–22)

More than merely a mode of transportation, the horse was recognized in Bible times as a symbol of strength in carrying warriors into battle. The horse is described in Proverbs 21:31 as a weapon of war: "The horse is prepared for the day of battle." In Zechariah 10:3, God metaphorically describes making Judah "His royal horse in battle." When people go to war, they need all the power they can get, and horses have the speed and muscle to transport soldiers where they are needed.

What kind of horse is described in Revelation 6? These are horses with riders "going out." The first horse went out "conquering and to conquer." The imagery is not of a lazy, slow horse pulling a wagon or of a child riding a pony through a pasture of flowers. The picture is of warfare. The horses are spirited and carry riders with an urgent message to share. God showed John powerful and swift horses carrying their riders to their destinations. No one will stop them.

Revelation shows us that our world is a battlefield between good and evil. There is a great war between Christ and Satan that began in heaven (Rev. 12:7). That war spilled over into the earth (Rev. 12:9; Luke 10:18). Revelation 12–14 depicts evil powers that are bent on destroying God's people. The vision described in these chapters contains a message of warning and preparation. It can readily be described by riders on horses going out into the entire world. The picture in Revelation 6 paints a scene of speed and warfare. Why are there *four* horses?

The Symbolic Number Four

There are many "fours" in Revelation 6. There are four living creatures, four horses, four colors of horses, four riders, and four messages. Is this a coincidence? Numbers hold meaning in the Bible, especially in apocalyptic literature like Revelation. Four is a symbolic number in the Bible, representing things that are "universal." Like the four points on a compass, the four horsemen go throughout the earth. They cover the globe. When Peter was given a vision to take the gospel to the Gentiles, a sheet with "four corners" was let down from heaven (Acts 10:11). Similarly, there are angels holding back the "four winds" from the "four corners of the earth" (Rev. 7:1). Thus, *four* represents universal truth that must go out everywhere. This number describes the worldwide work of the four horsemen who "went out" (Rev. 7:2) with their messages.

In order to begin to help us understand the pattern and meaning of the symbols in our study, we introduce a diagram on which we will place the truths we are learning. It will be based on four quadrants, which are a pattern repeated in the sanctuary and in Jesus' Parable of the Sower. The sanctuary and the parable reveal deeper truths about the four horsemen. At this point, we will simply place the four horsemen and their colors in the diagram. We will discuss the sanctuary and Jesus' parable in later chapters.

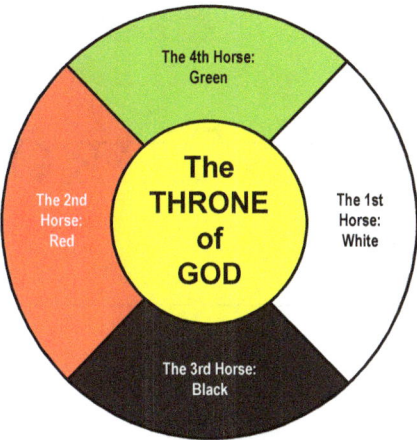

Many questions about the four horsemen remain. Where do they come from? What is their message? Why are they four different colors? Who are the four living creatures? What are the seals? To answer these questions, we need to review the setting of this part of Revelation by backing up to Revelation 4 and its depiction of the throne room of heaven.

Chapter 2

HEAVEN'S THRONE ROOM

What is it like to enter the throne room of a king? Perhaps you have some idea about it by having visited the office of a very important government official. On the other hand, maybe as a child in school you went to the principal's office to be disciplined. Did you enter with awe and wonder or with fear and trepidation? John in Revelation had the glorious experience of entering in vision the throne room of the universe. In this chapter, we will join him in feeling the heartbeat of all creation. It will provide a backdrop for us to understand more clearly the four horsemen of Revelation 6.

John's vision in Revelation 4 begins at the throne of God in the heavenly sanctuary. He is shown the role of God, the role of man's Representative, and the work of the servants of God. As we join John in looking at the scene of the final judgment of God, we are witnessing the final phase of the plan of salvation for man.

Daniel saw the scene that we are about to study. He sets the stage for us.

> I watched till thrones were put in place, and the Ancient of Days was seated; His garment was white as snow, and the hair of His head was like pure wool. His throne *was* a fiery flame, its wheels a burning fire; a fiery stream issued and came forth from before Him. A thousand thousands ministered to Him;

ten thousand times ten thousand stood before Him. The court was seated, and the books were opened (Dan. 7:9, 10).

Consider how John is invited to view the throne of God in heaven.

After these things I looked, and behold, a door standing open in heaven. And the first voice which I heard was like a trumpet speaking with me, saying, "Come up here, and I will show you things which must take place after this." Immediately I was in the Spirit ... (Rev. 4:1, 2)

Here John is invited to walk through an open door in heaven and is told that he will be shown future events.

And behold, a throne set in heaven, and One sat on the throne. And He who sat there was like a jasper and a sardius stone in appearance; and there was a rainbow around the throne, in appearance like an emerald. (Rev. 4:2, 3)

John sees a throne "set" in heaven. Then he sees God sit down on this throne. He describes God as a bright light with a red glow. There is a beautiful rainbow around the throne that gives the scene a greenish glow.

Elders and Living Creatures in the Throne Room (Revelation 4:4–11)

Who is in this throne room in heaven?

Around the throne were twenty-four thrones, and

> on the thrones I saw twenty-four elders sitting, clothed in white robes; and they had crowns of gold on their heads. (Rev. 4:4)

Around the throne of God, John sees twenty-four elders dressed in white and wearing crowns of gold. Who are these elders? Revelation 3:5 tells us, "He who overcomes shall be clothed in white garments" and in verse 21, "To him who overcomes I will grant to sit with Me on My throne, as I also overcame and sat down with My Father on His throne." These elders are apparently men from the earth who have overcome by the grace of Jesus. They wear symbols of victory over sin, and, in chapter 5, they sing a song of their redemption to God by Christ's blood "out of every tribe and tongue and people and nation" (Rev. 5:9, 10). They sit next to the throne of God. They are observing the works of God and are man's representatives in heaven. What else do we see in this throne room?

> And from the throne proceeded lightnings, thunderings, and voices. Seven lamps of fire were burning before the throne, which are the seven Spirits of God. Before the throne there was a sea of glass, like crystal. (Rev. 4:5, 6)

Before the throne of God, John sees a seven-candled lamp stand and a sea of glass like a crystal. These articles sound like articles in the earthly sanctuary. What an awesome scene it was to look upon! John's eyes must have been overwhelmed with the majesty before him. Can you imagine standing next to him looking into God's throne room? There are yet more strange and interesting things to see.

> ... And in the midst of the throne, and around the

> throne, were four living creatures full of eyes in front and in back. The first living creature was like a lion, the second living creature like a calf, the third living creature had a face like a man, and the fourth living creature was like a flying eagle. The four living creatures, each having six wings, were full of eyes around and within. And they do not rest day or night, saying: "Holy, holy, holy, Lord God Almighty, Who was and is and is to come!" Whenever the living creatures give glory and honor and thanks to Him who sits on the throne, who lives forever and ever ... (Rev. 4:6–9)

Who or what are these four creatures? Even though the King James Version uses the word "beasts" in these verses, "living creatures" is a more accurate translation from the Greek. John does not see wild, ferocious animals as we find in Revelation 13. These are symbolic living creatures.

- The first "living creature" is like a lion.
- The second "living creature" is like a calf.
- The third "living creature" is like a man.
- The fourth "living creature" is like a flying eagle.

These living creatures have a specific work in heaven and appear to be angels who stand next to God, ready to carry out His work. As they gaze upon the character and work of God, they are compelled to say, *Holy is He*. When they finish giving glory to God, John continues by describing the response of another group in heaven.

> ... the twenty-four elders fall down before Him who sits on the throne and worship Him who lives forever and ever, and cast their crowns before the throne, saying: "You are worthy, O Lord, to receive glory

and honor and power; for You created all things, and by Your will they exist and were created." (Rev. 4:10, 11)

We can place the symbols we have covered so far into a visual representation, as we see below.

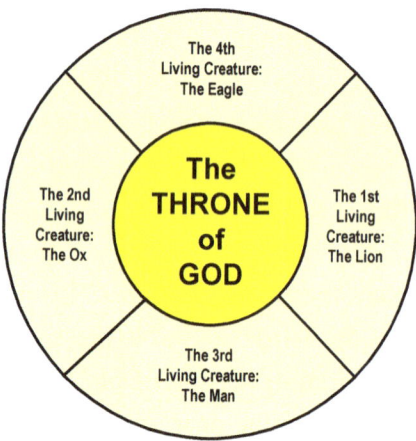

God's Throne Room is the Center of Communications

John is describing activities in the throne room of God. When the living creatures honor God, the twenty-four elders respond with words of thanksgiving. God is not alone. He is surrounded by intelligent beings—the twenty-four elders, the four living creatures, and thousands of angels. As we contemplate this scene in the heavenly sanctuary, we realize that John is describing those who are closest to God, in other words, God's immediate family. God's throne is not a lonely and quiet place. It is very busy and there is plenty of sound. In our mind's eye we can see "… from the throne proceeded lightnings, thundering, and voices" (Rev. 4:5).

Like the chambers of the House of Representatives or Parliament, many important decisions are made in the throne room of heaven. Then, like the switchboard of a busy telephone company, many communications come forth from the throne room as well. It is a place worth focusing our attention. From this central place of power, of God's residence, we are about to witness a problem in the throne room that only God can resolve. Turning to Revelation 5:1–6, we read:

> And I saw in the right hand of Him who sat on the throne a scroll written inside and on the back, sealed with seven seals. (Rev. 5:1)

John sees a book that is sealed with seven seals in the right hand of God the Father. What is written in that book? John writes:

> Then I saw a strong angel proclaiming with a loud voice, "Who is worthy to open the scroll and to loose its seals?" And no one in heaven or on the earth or under the earth was able to open the scroll, or to look at it. So I wept much, because no one was found worthy to open and read the scroll, or to look at it. (Rev. 5:2–4)

An angel asks a question: *Who is worthy—who has earned the right—to open the book with the seven seals?* John looks left and right and realizes that no one is answering the call. He begins to weep because no one has come forward to open the book. Suddenly, the scene changes.

> But one of the elders said to me, "Do not weep. Behold, the Lion of the tribe of Judah, the Root of David, has prevailed to open the scroll and to loose its seven seals." And I looked, and behold, in the midst of the throne and of the four living creatures,

> and in the midst of the elders, stood a Lamb as though it had been slain, having seven horns and seven eyes, which are the seven Spirits of God sent out into all the earth. (Rev. 5:5, 6)

John is comforted by one of the elders who tells him that the Lion of the tribe of Judah, the root of David, has earned the right to open the book. John turns to look and sees a Lamb which had been slain, standing before the throne of God. This Lamb has perfect power (as symbolized by *seven* horns) and perfect knowledge (as symbolized by *seven* eyes). Who is the Lamb that John sees in this vision? John identifies Him in his Gospel. "The next day John saw Jesus coming toward him, and said, 'Behold! The Lamb of God who takes away the sin of the world! …'" (John 1:29). The Lamb is Jesus. The utterance of this symbolic name for Jesus was prophetic. Christ became the Lamb of God when he was offered as the perfect sacrifice on the cross of Calvary for the sins of man. He is "the Lamb slain from the foundation of the world" (Rev. 13:8).

A Parallel in Hebrews

Yet, why is Jesus, the Lamb of God, standing before the throne of God in Revelation 5? Hebrews gives us an answer.

> Inasmuch then as the children have partaken of flesh and blood, He Himself likewise shared in the same, that through death He might destroy him who had the power of death, that is, the devil, and release those who through fear of death were all their lifetime subject to bondage. (Heb. 2:14, 15)

Jesus took flesh and blood because man sinned. The law of sin demands the life of the sinner. Christ became a man that He might offer His life as a substitute for man. Only by the sacrifice of

Himself as the Son of man, could the power of death be destroyed. Verse 16 adds, "For indeed He does not give aid to angels, but He does give aid to the seed of Abraham." As a man, Jesus did not use either His divine creative powers or the supernatural powers of an angel. He used the same powers available to all descendents of Abraham, including you and me.

> Therefore, in all things He had to be made like His brethren, that He might be a merciful and faithful High Priest in things pertaining to God, to make propitiation for the sins of the people. For in that He Himself has suffered, being tempted, He is able to aid those who are tempted. (Heb. 2:17, 18)

Christ became a man that He might serve man in the capacity of High Priest. As man's High Priest, Jesus could make the final reconciliation for the sins of the people, the final atonement for sin. Not only does Jesus ask God to forgive our sins, He is able to help those that are tempted. If we have faith in Jesus Christ, this sacrifice has set us free from the power of death. The sacrifice on the cross was not the last work of Jesus for man. Hebrews says that Jesus had to be a man "that he might be a merciful and faithful high priest in things pertaining to God, to make reconciliation for the sins of the people" (Heb. 2:17, KJV). Christ is right now doing the work of a high priest that man might be saved.

In just a bit, we will study more about His appointment as high priest, but first we need to understand a basic principle in Hebrews about the sanctuary. When God gave Moses instructions on how to build the sanctuary in the wilderness, God told him to be careful. "See that you make all things according to the pattern shown you on the mountain" (Heb. 8:5b). *Make everything in the earthly sanctuary as you have seen them in the heavenly sanctuary.* Now notice, all the revelations to Moses about the sanctuary on earth were to "serve the copy and shadow of the heavenly things" (Heb. 8:5a). In other words, what you see in the earthly sanctuary is a pattern of the way things operate in heaven. The sanctuary in Revelation 4 and 5 can, in the same way, be understood according to the sanctuary service on earth given to Israel through Moses. Jesus' role as the offering of propitiation and priest in Hebrews 2:14–17 parallels what He does as the Lamb of God in Revelation 5.

Jesus was called our "High Priest" in Hebrews for a very important reason. Consider how earthly high priests were called: "And no man takes this honor to himself, but he who is called by God, just as Aaron *was*" (Heb. 5:4). The call did not come from an earthly king with a royal declaration or a group of wise men assembled for the work of choosing the high priest. It is God who chooses: He chose Jesus Christ to be our High Priest for *the reconciliation of the atonement of sins*.

Only a high priest, as a representative of man, could make atonement for the sins of the people. Reconciliation was a special work. "But into the second part the high priest *went* alone once a year, not without blood, which he offered for himself and *for* the people's sins *committed* in ignorance" (Heb. 9:7). This special work happened only once a year on the Day of Atonement. The Jews called this a day of judgment. And the place of focus was the Most Holy Place. Reconciliation took place in that apartment.

The earthly day of atonement was a shadow of the heavenly day of atonement. This means that Revelation 5 is telling us about the Lamb of God removing sin from the sanctuary on the day of atonement. In this chapter Jesus functions as High Priest. Notice that the Lamb of God is standing before the throne of God in the heavenly sanctuary in this vision and that He takes the book and opens it. He is fulfilling His work as the Son of Man.

Herein is a major key to the understanding of Revelation 5. John's vision portrays the ceremony in the heavenly sanctuary in which God the Father recognized Jesus as the High Priest for man. Our High Priest in the heavenly sanctuary earned the right "to make reconciliation for the sins of the people" (Heb. 2:17, KJV). In Revelation 5, the Father allows Jesus the Lamb to come up to the throne and receive a book. As He opens the book, the final phase of reconciliation begins–the heavenly day of atonement.

Identifying the Book in Revelation 5

Returning to Revelation 5 and picking up with verse 7, we read: "Then He came and took the scroll out of the right hand of Him who sat on the throne." John sees Jesus, the Lamb of God, who is the son of Man, walking up to the throne and taking a scroll, or book (KJV, Greek *biblion*), from God the Father. This "scroll," with the seven seals, is the only book that the Lamb is said to have received. What is this book? Notice the reference to a "book" that belongs to the Lamb in Revelation 13: "All who dwell on the earth will worship him, whose names have not been written in the Book of Life of the Lamb slain from the foundation of the world" (Rev. 13:8). This Book of Life is also mentioned in Revelation 3:5; 17:8; 20:12, 15; 21:27; 22:19; and, by Paul, in Philippians 4:3. In Revelation 21:27, it is again described as "the Lamb's Book of Life." It contains the names of those who will enter heaven. Remarkably, Revelation 17:8 says that the names in it were written "from the foundation of the world," and Revelation 3:5 says that names in it can not be blotted out. Those whose names are not written in this book will not enter heaven. This book is very important! It calls to mind the words of the old gospel song, "Is my name written there?"

What happens after Christ takes this book? Continuing in Revelation 5, we read:

> Now when He had taken the scroll, the four living creatures and the twenty-four elders fell down before

> the Lamb, each having a harp, and golden bowls full of incense, which are the prayers of the saints. And they sang a new song, saying: "You are worthy to take the scroll, and to open its seals; for You were slain, and have redeemed us to God by Your blood out of every tribe and tongue and people and nation, and have made us kings and priests to our God; and we shall reign on the earth." (Rev. 5:8–10)

The living creatures and elders recognize the significance of the Lamb taking the book. They bow down and worship the Lamb of God. Notice that the elders have harps and censors like the priests of the earthly sanctuary. The elders also sing a new song that has not been sung before. In this new song, they declare that the Lamb is worthy to take the book from God the Father. It is a song that we can sing too. Jesus has redeemed us to God by His precious blood and has made us kings and priests who will reign on earth. The elders praise Jesus for giving His life for them.

Hebrews helps us understand the praise that comes from the elders. Paul wrote Hebrews so we might understand that Jesus Christ, the Son of man, earned the right to be our sacrifice on Calvary and to stand as our intercessor, our High Priest, in heaven before the throne of God.

> But Christ came as High Priest of the good things to come, with the greater and more perfect tabernacle not made with hands, that is, not of this creation. Not with the blood of goats and calves, but with His own blood He entered the Most Holy Place once for all, having obtained eternal redemption. For if the blood of bulls and goats and the ashes of a heifer, sprinkling the unclean, sanctifies for the purifying of the flesh, how much more shall the blood of Christ,

> who through the eternal Spirit offered Himself without spot to God, cleanse your conscience from dead works to serve the living God? And for this reason He is the Mediator of the new covenant, by means of death, for the redemption of the transgressions under the first covenant, that those who are called may receive the promise of the eternal inheritance. (Heb. 9:11–15)

Christ is our High Priest in the heavenly sanctuary. Jesus paid the penalty for our sin with His own precious blood. Because of the sacrificed blood on the cross by the Lamb of God, our sins were forgiven and covered in the Lamb's Book of Life. On the day of atonement in the heavenly sanctuary, our High Priest will remove these sins forevermore. This service by our Redeemer entitles us to receive the promise of eternal inheritance.

Response of the Universe (Revelation 5:11–14)

Revelation 5 portrays the rest of heaven observing the Lamb before the throne, and it records their response.

> Then I looked, and I heard the voice of many angels around the throne, the living creatures, and the elders; and the number of them was ten thousand times ten thousand, and thousands of thousands, saying with a loud voice: "Worthy is the Lamb who was slain to receive power and riches and wisdom, and strength and honor and glory and blessing!" (Rev. 5:11, 12)

After this, the praise to the Lamb of God reaches a new crescendo. All the angels around the throne, the living creatures, and the elders all raise their voice in praise.

> And every creature which is in heaven and on the earth and under the earth and such as are in the sea, and all that are in them, I heard saying: "Blessing and honor and glory and power be to Him who sits on the throne, and to the Lamb, forever and ever!" Then the four living creatures said, "Amen!" And the twenty-four elders fell down and worshiped Him who lives forever and ever. (Rev. 5:13, 14)

The praise of the elders is echoed by praise from the angels of God. Then praise for the Lamb of God comes from every creature in heaven and earth. It is as if the whole universe erupts into praise for the Lamb who takes the Book of Life.

Summary

We have discovered that Revelation 4 and 5 describe an event that takes place in heaven. John sees God the Father sitting on a throne, surrounded by elders and living creatures. There is a book in God's right hand. John then sees the Lamb of God take the book. What is going on here? Why does God call John up to heaven to witness this event? What is this event? When did it happen? God spoke in vision to another messenger. In our next chapter we will examine the heavenly sanctuary through what she saw.

Chapter 3

Another View of the Heavenly Sanctuary

As we move through Revelation 4 and 5 to understand the context of Revelation 6 and the four horsemen, we must take time to consider what Christ is doing in the throne room of heaven. One of Ellen White's earliest visions helps explain what John recorded in Revelation 4 and 5. In the book *Early Writings*, she describes what she saw. As you read this vision, ask yourself: *What is she seeing? Does it sound like what we have been studying?*

> I saw a throne, and on it sat the Father and the Son. I gazed on Jesus' countenance and admired His lovely person ... Before the throne I saw the Advent people— the church and the world. I saw two companies, one bowed down before the throne, deeply interested, while the other stood uninterested and careless ... (*Early Writings*, p. 54)

Notice in her vision that the Father and the Son are both sitting on the same throne in the heavenly sanctuary. In Revelation 3:21, Jesus spoke of His being seated on His Father's throne. What does she see happening next?

I saw the Father rise from the throne, and in a flaming chariot go into the holy of holies within the veil, and sit down. Then Jesus rose up from the throne, and the most of those who were bowed down arose with Him ... Those who arose when Jesus did, kept their eyes fixed on Him as He left the throne and led them out a little way. Then He raised His right arm, and we heard His lovely voice saying, "Wait here; I am going to My Father to receive the kingdom; keep your garments spotless, and in a little while I will return from the wedding and receive you to Myself." Then a cloudy chariot, with wheels like flaming fire, surrounded by angels, came to where Jesus was. He stepped into the chariot and was borne to the holiest, where the Father sat. There I beheld Jesus, a great High Priest, standing before the Father. (*Early Writings*, p. 55)

Ellen White describes the Father rising from the throne and traveling by flaming chariot into the Holy of Holies in the heavenly sanctuary. There He took His seat upon another throne. She then describes Jesus rising from the same throne, where He and the Father had been sitting, and traveling by flaming chariot into the Holiest before the Father. There He stood before the Father in the garments of a great high priest. What event was Ellen White seeing?

Insights from Hebrews

I would like to break away from Ellen White's vision for a moment and turn our attention to Hebrews, where, in chapter 8, Paul also describes the Father and the Son sitting in heaven.

Now this is the main point of the things we are

saying: We have such a High Priest, who is seated at the right hand of the throne of the Majesty in the heavens, a Minister of the sanctuary and of the true tabernacle which the Lord erected, and not man. (Heb. 8:1, 2)

Just as Jesus is seated with the Father in the scene in Ellen White's vision, so is He, as our High Priest, *"seated* at the right hand of the throne of the Majesty in the heavens" as stated in Hebrews. As we move to chapter 9, Hebrews goes into greater detail about the earthly sanctuary, a shadow of the heavenly one. It explains its different apartments and what they were used for.

Then indeed, even the first covenant had ordinances of divine service and the earthly sanctuary. For a tabernacle was prepared: the first part, in which was the lampstand, the table, and the showbread, which is called the sanctuary; and behind the second veil, the part of the tabernacle which is called the Holiest of All, which had the golden censer and the ark of the covenant overlaid on all sides with gold, in which were the golden pot that had the manna, Aaron's rod that budded, and the tablets of the covenant; and above it were the cherubim of glory overshadowing the mercy seat. Of these things we cannot now speak in detail. Now when these things had been thus prepared, the priests always went into the first part of the tabernacle, performing the services. But into the second part the high priest went alone once a year, not without blood, which he offered for himself and for the people's sins committed in ignorance. (Heb. 9:1–7)

In this description we see that the candlestick and the table of showbread were in the first apartment of the sanctuary, known as the Holy Place. In the second apartment, known as the Most Holy Place, was the Ark of the Covenant. The golden censer was associated with the Most Holy Place.

The *daily* work of the priests took place in the Holy Place. The *yearly* work of the high priest took place in the Most Holy Place, as Paul says: "But into the second part the high priest *went* alone once a year" (Heb. 9:7). Hebrews describes the apartments of the earthly sanctuary, saying they were a "copy and shadow of the heavenly things …" (Heb. 8:5). Notice how Paul brings this out.

> For Christ has not entered the holy places made with hands, which are copies of the true, but into heaven itself, now to appear in the presence of God for us; not that He should offer Himself often, as the high priest enters the Most Holy Place every year with blood of another—He then would have had to suffer often since the foundation of the world; but now, once at the end of the ages, He has appeared to put away sin by the sacrifice of Himself. And as it is appointed for men to die once, but after this the judgment, so Christ was offered once to bear the sins of many. To those who eagerly wait for Him He will appear a second time, apart from sin, for salvation. (Heb. 9:24–28)

When Jesus returned to heaven, He entered the Holy Place of the sanctuary to appear before God for us as our heavenly High Priest. Notice Paul's statement in verse 26, "but now, once at the end of the ages [or, as the King James Version reads, "Now once in *the end of the world*"], He has appeared to put away sin by the sacrifice of Himself." What does this mean? Paul is describing the final phase of Jesus' ministry for the redemption of man, which includes Christ's moving from the Holy Place of the heavenly sanctuary into the Most Holy Place. When He moves to the Most Holy Place, He begins the task that corresponds to the work of the high priest, when he entered the Most Holy Place once a year (Heb. 9:7) on the Day of Atonement.

The description of Hebrews 9:26 matches the description of Revelation 5. It summarizes the message of John's vision of the heavenly throne room. The Lamb of God before God's throne taking the book is none other than Jesus Christ, our great High Priest, coming before God the Father on the day of atonement to put away sin forever.

Returning to Ellen White's Vision

These descriptions also line up with Ellen White's vision. They each describe the Most Holy Place and Christ's work as high priest in putting away sin. They all speak of the time of the end and the day of atonement, which take place before the Second Coming of Christ.

Ellen White tells us that she saw both the Father and the Son sitting on a throne in heaven. Then she saw that the Father and Jesus were taken, one by one, in fiery chariots, from the throne to the Most Holy Place in the Sanctuary. In the Holy of Holies, she saw God seated on a throne and Jesus standing before the Father and acting as High Priest.

As we consider this scene, let us ask ourselves some questions: *What does the sanctuary in heaven look like?* Revelation 4 and 5 depict it as being arranged like the one that Moses constructed in the wilderness. Paul's description parallels this as well. In knowing what the earthly sanctuary looked like, we can visualize the sanctuary in heaven. *What does it mean that Jesus is ministering for us in the heavenly sanctuary? What work is He doing right now?* Ellen White tells us "… important truths concerning the heavenly sanctuary and the great work there carried forward for man's redemption were taught by the earthly sanctuary and its services" (*The Great Controversy*, p. 414). What are these "important truths"?

The earthly sanctuary teaches two important truths. It shows us God's tremendous love for fallen mankind, and it reveals that, for God to be both merciful and just, the plan of redemption requires sacrifice. The portrayal of the heavenly sanctuary and its services in Revelation reveals God's total transparency. When you view the throne room of heaven, you see the Lord of the universe surrounded by special angels and the twenty-four elders. All of God's work is open to the inhabitants of heaven and earth.

Now let us look more carefully at the two main services of the earthly sanctuary. This will help us understand the work that Jesus is doing right now in the heavenly sanctuary. Ellen White insightfully wrote:

> The ministration of the earthly sanctuary consisted of two divisions; *the priests* ministered daily in the holy place, while once a year *the high priest* performed a special work of atonement in the most holy, for the cleansing of the sanctuary. Day by day the repentant sinner brought his offering to the door of the tabernacle and, placing his hand upon the victim's head, *confessed his sins*, thus in figure transferring them from himself to the innocent sacrifice. The animal was then slain. "Without shedding of blood," says the apostle, there is no remission of sin. [Heb. 9:22.] "The life of the flesh is in the blood." Leviticus 17:11. The broken law of God demanded the life of the transgressor. The blood, representing the forfeited life of the sinner, whose guilt the victim bore, was carried by *the priest* into the holy place and sprinkled before the veil, behind

which was the ark containing the law that the sinner had transgressed. By this ceremony the sin was, through the blood, transferred in figure to the sanctuary. In some cases the blood was not taken into the holy place; but the flesh was then to be eaten by the priest, as Moses directed the sons of Aaron, saying: "God hath given it you to bear the iniquity of the congregation." Leviticus 10:17. Both ceremonies alike symbolized the transfer of the sin from the penitent to the sanctuary. (*The Great Controversy*, p. 418, emphasis supplied)

The ministration of the earthly sanctuary had two parts: the *daily* ministry of the priests in the Holy Place, and the special work of atonement in the Most Holy Place for the cleansing of the sanctuary performed *once a year* by the high priest.

Steps to Take if You Sin, Symbolized in the Daily Ministry

What was required of a man if he sinned against the Lord during the time of the earthly sanctuary? When a man sinned against God's law, the plan of redemption required him to present himself at the sanctuary with a sacrifice. Then, he was to place his hands on the head of the sacrifice and confess his sin. This action symbolized the transfer of sin from the sinner to the sacrifice. After this, the repentant sinner cut the throat of the sacrifice. The death of the sacrificial animal symbolized the forfeited life of the sinner in payment for sin. If the sinner was a priest or if the whole congregation was guilty of sin, the blood of the sacrifice was carried by the priest into the sanctuary and sprinkled before the veil in the Holy Place (Lev. 4:4–6, 13–17). If the sinner was a common person, the blood of the sacrifice was put on the horns of the altar of burnt offering (Lev. 4:30). The sin of the repentant one, represented by the blood, was transferred in figure to the sanctuary. The blood "made atonement" for the confessed sin of the repentant sinner (Lev. 4:20, 26, 31, 35).

> Such was the work that went on, day by day, throughout the year. The sins of Israel were thus transferred to the sanctuary, and a special work became necessary for their removal. God commanded that an atonement be made for each of the sacred apartments.... An atonement was also to be made for the altar, to "cleanse it, and hallow it from the uncleanness of the children of Israel." Leviticus 16:16, 19. (*The Great Controversy*, p. 418)

God had provided a way for fallen humans to return to Him. He taught His people that sin results in death, yet men can be reconciled to Him through the blood of an innocent sacrifice. Though the transgressor was spiritually dead in sin, the sprinkled blood of the sacrifice enabled him to stand born again before God. Yet, the story of redemption does not end with the confession of sin and the spilling of sacrificial blood. God instituted the Day of Atonement that men might realize that sin needs to be removed from the sanctuary for reconciliation in the sanctuary to be complete.

> The blood of Christ, while it was to release the repentant sinner from the condemnation of the law, was not to cancel the sin; it would stand on record in the sanctuary until the final atonement; so in the type the blood of the sin offering removed the sin from the penitent, but it rested in the sanctuary until the Day of Atonement. (*Patriarchs and Prophets*, p. 357)

The Day of Atonement: The Yearly

God's people need to understand something more about the removal of sin from the sanctuary. This is taught through the work of the high priest in the yearly service called the Day of Atonement.

> Once a year, on the great Day of Atonement, the [high] priest entered the most holy place for the cleansing of the sanctuary. The work there performed completed the yearly round of ministration. On the Day of Atonement two kids of the goats were brought to the door of the tabernacle, and lots were cast upon them, "one lot for the Lord, and the other lot for the scapegoat." [Leviticus 16:8.] The goat upon which fell the lot for the Lord was to be slain as a sin offering for the people. And the [high] priest was to bring his blood within the veil and sprinkle it upon the mercy seat and before the mercy seat ... (*The Great Controversy*, p. 419)

The high priest sprinkled the mercy seat with the blood of the goat in the Most Holy Place of the earthly sanctuary on this special Day of Atonement. Leslie Hardinge writes about the meaning of this act: : "Because these recorded sins had defiled the Tabernacle, his act of sprinkling them with blood had 'hallowed' and cleansed the edifice, and thus, symbolically had removed the records of every confessed and forgiven sin" (Leslie Hardinge, *With Jesus in His Sanctuary: A Walk Through the Tabernacle Along His Way*, p. 515).

What happened to all the confessed and forgiven sins of the people of God? Regarding the high priest, Hardinge explains: "As the divinely authorized representative of his people, he had paid the ransom price in blood for the confessed and forgiven sins of every participating Israelite, and now held them, as it were, in his personal possession" (Leslie Hardinge, *With Jesus in His Sanctuary*, p. 517).

What did the high priest do next? Hardinge writes: "His next task was to dispose of them symbolically in God's appointed way. Striding up to Azazel's goat he laid his hands on its head and thus placed all the confessed and forgiven sins of God's people upon him" (Leslie Hardinge, *With Jesus in His Sanctuary*, p. 517).

God's instructions to Moses tell us how the high priest was to remove sin from the sanctuary.

> Then Aaron shall cast lots for the two goats: one lot for the Lord and the other lot for the scapegoat. ... Aaron shall lay both his hands on the head of the live goat, confess over it all the iniquities of the children of Israel, and all their transgressions, concerning all their sins, putting them on the head of the goat, and shall send it away into the wilderness by the hand of a suitable man. The goat shall bear on itself all their iniquities to an uninhabited land; and he shall release the goat in the wilderness. (Lev. 16:8, 21, 22)

This ceremony took place on the special day that God set aside for the removal of sin from the sanctuary, called the Day of Atonement, which is in Hebrew *Yom Kippur*. On that day, a chosen man—the high priest—entered the Most Holy Place of the sanctuary to sprinkle the blood of the sacrifices of a bullock and the Lord's goat over the mercy seat of the Ark of the Covenant and before the mercy seat (Lev. 16:14, 15). God accepted the sacrifice of animals as a substitute for the confessed sinner. The act of sprinkling was a shadow of the heavenly work of Jesus. The sprinkled blood of the goat symbolized the blood of the perfect sacrifice of the Son of Man that was to be spilled on Calvary and that would be offered on the day of atonement in heaven.

After the high priest sprinkled the blood of the sacrifice in the Most Holy Place, he then left the sanctuary, where he applied it to the horns of the altar of sacrifice (Lev. 16:18). The blood within the veil and upon the altar of sacrifice symbolized the recording in heaven of the payment for sins, but it also symbolized the act of the high priest removing the sins that had been carried into the Holy Place in the daily services. All the sins that had been carried there during the year were transferred to the high priest. When the high priest had finished in the sanctuary and poured out the remaining sacrificial blood at the altar, he walked over to the scapegoat waiting in the court, placed his hands on its head, and confessed all the sins of Israel. This act symbolized the transfer of the sins from him to the goat. The goat was then led into the wilderness, a land not inhabited. The sins that had separated God and man were removed from the sanctuary. God and man were reconciled. The people then celebrated their reunion with a feast.

Why did God institute the earthly sanctuary service?

> The whole ceremony was designed to impress the Israelites with the holiness of God and His abhorrence of sin; and, further, to show them that they could not come in contact with sin without becoming polluted. Every man was required to afflict his soul while this work of atonement was going forward. All business was to be laid aside, and the whole congregation of Israel were to spend the day in solemn humiliation before God, with prayer, fasting, and deep searching of heart. (*The Great Controversy*, p. 419)

What did God teach His children through the services of the sanctuary?

Important truths concerning the atonement are taught by the typical service. A substitute was accepted in the sinner's stead; but the sin was not canceled by the blood of the victim. A means was thus provided by which it was transferred to the sanctuary. By the offering of blood the sinner acknowledged the authority of the law, confessed his guilt in transgression, and expressed his desire for pardon through faith in a Redeemer to come; but he was not yet entirely released from the condemnation of the law. On the Day of Atonement the high priest, having taken an offering from the congregation, went into the most holy place with the blood of this offering, and sprinkled it upon the mercy seat, directly over the law, to make satisfaction for its claims. Then, in his character of mediator, he took the sins upon himself and bore them from the sanctuary. Placing his hands upon the head of the scape goat, he confessed over him all these sins, thus in figure transferring them from himself to the goat. The goat then bore them away, and they were regarded as forever separated from the people. (*The Great Controversy*, p. 420)

The sanctuary taught men the road to redemption. Why did God have Moses build an earthly sanctuary? Remember Hebrews 8:5? The earthly sanctuary was both a "copy" and a foreshadowing of heavenly things. It teaches that sin destroys the relationship between God and man. It causes death. Yet, God gave us a way out by giving us His Son as a sacrifice for our sins that we might take the character of Jesus as ours. The removal of sin from the heavenly sanctuary, by our great High Priest, is the only way God can vindicate the Law and demonstrate mercy for fallen man. Ellen White tells us, "His ministry in the sanctuary in heaven was the great object that cast its shadow backward and made clear the ministry of the Jewish priesthood" (*The Acts of the Apostles*, p. 246).

> Therefore, in all things He had to be made like His brethren, that He might be a merciful and faithful High Priest in things pertaining to God, to make propitiation for the sins of the people. For in that He Himself has suffered, being tempted, He is able to aid those who are tempted. (Heb. 2:17, 18)

Jesus became a man that He might do the work of a man in saving man. Christ has been ministering as our High Priest ever since He returned to heaven. Is this important for us to understand today?

> For eighteen centuries this work of ministration continued in the first apartment of the sanctuary. The blood of Christ, pleaded in behalf of penitent believers, secured their pardon and acceptance with the Father, yet their sins still remained upon the books of record. As in the typical service there was a work of atonement at the close of the year, so before Christ's work for the redemption of men is completed there is a work of atonement for the removal of sin from the sanctuary. This is the service which began when the 2300 days ended. At that time, as foretold by Daniel the prophet, our High Priest entered the most holy, to perform the last division of His solemn work,—to cleanse the sanctuary. (*The Great Controversy*, p. 421)

Our sins are on the books of heaven, but they have been covered by the blood of the Lamb. Hebrews describes the inauguration of the earthly sanctuary and teaches that, as the earthly sanctuary required the purification of blood, so would the heavenly "holy places" likewise need to be purified by the blood of sacrifice (Heb. 9:23). In a similar way, as the wilderness sanctuary was cleansed, so the heavenly sanctuary will be cleansed. Daniel has given us the reference point. "And he said to me, 'For two thousand three hundred days; then the sanctuary shall be cleansed'" (Dan. 8:14). The "two thousand and three hundred days" means 2,300 instances of the Day of Atonement. Since the Day of Atonement came once a year, this 2,300-day prophecy means 2,300 years. At the end of the 2,300 Days of Atonement, or 2,300 years, our High Priest entered the Most Holy Place in heaven to begin His final work of cleansing the sanctuary in heaven.

> As anciently the sins of the people were by faith placed upon the sin offering and through its blood transferred, in figure, to the earthly sanctuary, so in *the new covenant* the sins of the repentant are by faith placed upon Christ and transferred, in fact, to the heavenly sanctuary. And as the typical cleansing of the earthly was accomplished by the removal of the sins by which it had been polluted, so the actual cleansing of the heavenly is to be accomplished by the removal, or blotting out, of the sins which are there recorded. But before this can be accomplished, there must be an examination of the books of record to determine who, through repentance of sin and faith in Christ, are entitled to the benefits of His atonement. The cleansing of the sanctuary therefore involves a work of investigation—a work of judgment. This work must be performed prior to the coming of Christ to redeem His people; for when He comes, *His reward is with Him to give to*

> *every man according to his works.* Revelation 22:12.
> (*The Great Controversy*, p. 421, emphasis supplied)

This final work of our High Priest Jesus Christ, the removal or blotting out of the sins of man, is now going on. When this final work of judgment is finished, He will return to earth to gather His children. Daniel described this event, which began at the end of the 2,300-day prophecy.

> I watched till thrones were put in place, and the Ancient of Days was seated ... The court was seated, and the books were opened. (Dan. 7:9, 10)

We can now say that when the judgment was set in the heavenly sanctuary, the Lion of the tribe of Judah took the book of life from the right hand of God and opened it so that it could be used in the investigative judgment. This is the action anticipated in Revelation 4 and 5. Let us read from Hebrews 9, which culminates in the heavenly day of atonement.

> For Christ has not entered the holy places made with hands, which are copies of the true, but into heaven itself, now to appear in the presence of God for us. (Heb. 9:24)

Ever since He ascended into heaven, our High Priest has been ministering or interceding for us before God the Father in the Holy Place of the heavenly sanctuary.

> Not that He should offer Himself often, as the high priest enters the Most Holy Place every year with blood of another—He then would have had to suffer often since the foundation of the world; but now,

once at the end of the ages, He has appeared to put away sin by the sacrifice of Himself. (Heb. 9:25, 26)

At the end of the 2,300 year prophecy in 1844, Jesus Christ, as our High Priest, went from the Holy Place to the Most Holy Place of the heavenly sanctuary to carry out the work of atonement that will "put away sin" forever. Hebrews says: "And as it is appointed for men to die once, but after this the judgment ..." (Heb. 9:27).

Jesus Christ, our Great High Priest, entered the Most Holy Place in the heavenly sanctuary in 1844 to begin His final work of reconciliation in the plan of salvation for man. Paul understood this principle. Ellen White understood this principle, and John saw this principle and wrote about it in Revelation 4 and 5. What work does God want us to do before the Second Coming?

While the investigative judgment is going forward in heaven, while the sins of penitent believers are being removed from the sanctuary, there is to be a special work of purification, of putting away of sin, among God's people upon earth. This work is more clearly presented in the messages of Revelation 14. (*The Great Controversy*, p. 425)

Have you ever considered that God has a special work for you as an individual to accomplish before He comes again?

The condition of the unbelieving Jews illustrates the condition of the careless and unbelieving among professed Christians, who are willingly ignorant of the work of our merciful High Priest. In the typical service, when the high priest entered the most holy place, all Israel were required to gather about the sanctuary and in the most solemn manner humble their souls before God, that they might receive the pardon of their sins and not be cut off from the congregation. How much more essential in this antitypical Day of Atonement that we understand the work of our High Priest and know what duties are required of us. (*The Great Controversy*, p. 430)

What was required of the children of Israel during the time their high priest was in the Most Holy Place on the Day of Atonement? They were to gather themselves around the sanctuary. They were asked to humble themselves before their Creator. They were to examine their lives. What will happen to the careless and unbelieving professed Christians who are willingly ignorant of the work of our High Priest in the heavenly sanctuary today? They will not receive pardon for their sins.

We are living in the last days. It is essential for us today to understand the work of Jesus Christ, our High Priest, in the heavenly sanctuary and what our duty is. May our hearts be broken and become receptive to the Holy Spirit in preparation for the end of time that we may accept the message of the gospel.

Chapter 4

Creatures Around God's Throne and a Book Unsealed

Revelation is a book filled with meaningful symbols. Nonetheless, if we are not careful, we may get distracted by the details of the symbols and miss the vital message of the book. In this chapter we will look at the seals and the four "beasts" (KJV) in Revelation 4 and 6, and we will seek to understand more clearly what these strange creatures represent.

Seven Seals

The sixth chapter of Revelation tells us about seven seals that are around the book of life. The first four seals are associated with four horses and their riders. The fifth seal tells us that some of the children of God have been sacrificed for the word of God and for their testimony. The sixth seal tells us about the condition of the earth and of the men on the earth at the second coming of Jesus. Then we come to the last seal. The seventh seal is profound. We find it in Revelation 8:1: "When He opened the seventh seal, there was silence in heaven for about half an hour."

After reading about all the activity around God's throne room and seeing "lightning" and hearing "thundering and voices"

(Rev. 4:5) as well as the four living creatures and twenty-four elders continually worshiping and praising God (Rev. 4:9–11), it is a curious thing that John would describe there being "silence in heaven." That there is silence tells us that a change has taken place. What could this be? Can you imagine the solemnity of silence at the throne of God in heaven?

As our High Priest, Jesus has a special work in the heavenly sanctuary. He is judging every man and woman who has lived on this earth according to his or her works. When Christ finishes this work He will come back to earth to gather His children. John's vision of four riders, persecuted martyrs, and events just before the Second Coming all lead up to this verse about "silence" in heaven. What message does this have for us today?

The Living Creatures

Before we answer these questions, we need to understand more about these four "living creatures" who are closest to God's throne and who will later introduce the four horses in Revelation 6. Who are these "living creatures"? What is their relationship to the throne of God? Why are they the ones to introduce the four horses? What do the four horses have to do with us? For answers to these questions, we need to go back to Revelation 4 and read how God introduces the four "living creatures."

> Before the throne there was a sea of glass, like crystal. And in the midst of the throne, and around the throne, were four living creatures full of eyes in front and in back. (Rev. 4:6)

The King James Version uses the word "beasts" to describe the four living creatures. With our modern use of "beast," this would imply that they are ferocious animals. That is not John's intent. *Strong's Exhaustive Concordance* translates the Greek word *zōon*, which lies behind this term, as "a *live* thing, i.e. an *animal*." The *Seventh-day Adventist Bible Commentary*, vol. 7, p. 768, speaks of them being "living beings." Most translations use the words "living creatures." However we understand this term, we need to remember it is used symbolically to represent the "living being" who serves God in the center of the universe.

> The first living creature was like a lion, the second living creature like a calf, the third living creature had a face like a man, and the fourth living creature was like a flying eagle. The four living creatures, each having six wings, were full of eyes around and within. And they do not rest day or night, saying: "Holy, holy, holy, Lord God Almighty, Who was and is and is to come!" (Rev. 4:7, 8)

John introduces them in a specific order (first, second, third, and fourth). That they are full of eyes and that they praise the Lord points to their being intelligent beings. They look, act, and talk like angels. These "living creatures" closely resemble the "living creatures" described in Ezekiel 1:5–26, and share common characteristics with the *cherubim* in Ezekiel 10:1–20. The *seraphim* of Isaiah 6:2 likewise have six wings and sing "holy, holy, holy."

The Relation of the Four Creatures to the Standards of Israel

Let us turn to Numbers 2 to continue our study of the "living creatures" and their work in the heavenly sanctuary. We find that God placed the tribes of Israel in a certain order around the wilderness sanctuary.

> And on *the east side* toward the rising of the sun shall they of the standard of the camp of Judah pitch

throughout their armies ... On *the south side* shall be the standard of the camp of Reuben according to their armies ... On *the west side* shall be the standard of the camp of Ephraim according to their armies ... The standard of the camp of Dan shall be on *the north side* by their armies ... (Num. 2:3, 10, 18, 25, emphasis added)

Moses tells us that God put the camp of Judah on the east of the sanctuary, Reuben to the south, Ephraim to the west, and Dan on the north. Each tribe had a "standard" or banner about which the tribes were to camp. Numbers 2 does not tell us what figures or pictures were on these banners, but Leslie Hardinge, a life-long student of the sanctuary, draws from the distinguished Jewish scholar of the Middle Ages, Ibn Ezra, to describe the symbolic figures on their flags.

On the east rose the standard of the prince of Judah emblazoned with a *lion* (Gen 49:9; Rev 5:5). ... To the south (Num 2:10–16) fluttered the flag of Reuben, showing the figure of a *man* (Deut 33:6). ... To the west ... [was] Ephraim, his sign displaying an *ox* (Deut 33:16, 17). To the north (Num 2:25–31) Dan was encamped by his flag portraying a flying *eagle* killing a serpent (Gen 49:16). (Leslie Hardinge, *With Jesus in His Sanctuary*, p. 18, emphasis supplied)

We can diagram the orientation of the four primary standards of the tribes of Israel to the wilderness sanctuary as follows:

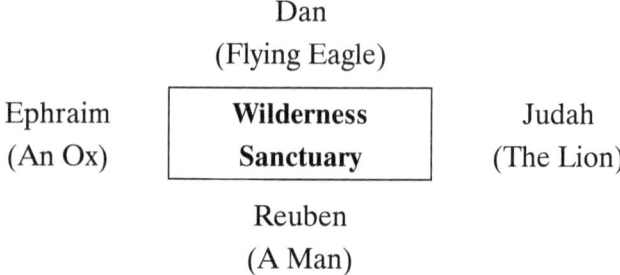

Why did God place these tribes in this order? Was it purely accidental, or is there a message we can learn from this placement? Our God is a God of knowledge and wisdom; He had reasons for the distribution of the tribes of Israel. James wrote: "Every good gift and every perfect gift is from above, and comes down from the Father of lights, with whom there is no variation or shadow of turning" (James 1:7). The wilderness sanctuary is a gift from God to teach us about salvation. The Bible has messages to reveal if we dig deeply. What can we learn in this instance?

Notice how Ellen White draws attention to the lessons in the wilderness.

> Precious were the lessons taught to Israel during their sojourn at Sinai. This was a period of special training for the inheritance of Canaan. And their surroundings here were favorable for the accomplishing of God's purpose. On the summit of Sinai, overshadowing the plain where the people spread their tents, rested the pillar of cloud which had been the guide of their journey. A pillar of fire by night, it assured them of the divine protection; and while they were locked in slumber, the bread of heaven fell gently upon the encampment ... Here, by the manifestation of His glory, God sought to impress Israel with the holiness of His character and requirements, and the exceeding guilt of transgression. (*Education*, p. 34)

Lessons from the children of Israel, as they traveled to the earthly Promised Land will shed light on our own journey to the heavenly Canaan. Dr. Hardinge continues with his explanation of the standards.

> These four likenesses are symbols to direct our attention to the four divisions of the twelve tribes of Israel encamped as a hollow square around the Tabernacle (Num 2:3-34). ...These four faces on the ensigns of these sectional leaders of Israel, represented all God's organized covenant people. ... The four idealized symbols of the rulers of ancient Israel arranged around the desert Tabernacle exhibited these characteristics of their Saviour. They were the representatives of all God's people who constitute the body of Christ in the world. "The church on earth, composed of those who are faithful and loyal to God, is the 'true tabernacle.' ... This tabernacle is Christ's body, and from north, south, east and west He gathers those who shall compose it" (7BC 931). (Leslie Hardinge, *With Jesus in His Sanctuary*, pp. 210, 211)

What are the characteristics of our Savior? Christ has the strength and commanding character of the lion, the power to finish each task like an ox, and the necessary knowledge and wisdom of the flying eagle. He also has tasted death like a man for all the children of the earth. His characteristics are sufficient to save us amply, fully, and entirely. God intends that we reflect the character of Christ. The attributes on these standards are also to represent our lives.

The Connection between the Earthly and Heavenly Sanctuaries

As the Israelites sojourn in the wilderness is parallel to our own journey to heaven, so also is the earthly sanctuary parallel to the heavenly sanctuary.

> But Christ came as High Priest of the good things to come, with the greater and more perfect tabernacle not made with hands, that is, not of this creation. (Heb. 9:11)

Ellen White expands on the significance of north, south, east, and west:

> This tabernacle is Christ's body, and from north, south, east, and west. He gathers those who shall help to compose it. ... A holy tabernacle is built up of those who receive Christ as their personal Saviour. ... Christ is the Minister of the true tabernacle, the High Priest of all who believe in Him as a personal Saviour. (*Signs of the Times*, Feb. 14, 1900)

What can we learn about the description of the heavenly sanctuary and throne room in Revelation 4 and 5 from looking at the earthly sanctuary? Drawing on Ezekiel 10:14, Hardinge tells us our High Priest in the heavenly sanctuary is surrounded by "the cherubim ... Each had the faces of a man, a lion, an ox and an eagle" (Leslie Hardinge, *With Jesus in His Sanctuary*, pp. 209, 210). We learned that in the earthly sanctuary, "These four likenesses are symbols to direct our attention to the four divisions of the twelve tribes of Israel encamped as a hollow square around the Tabernacle (Num. 2:3–34)" (Leslie Hardinge, *With Jesus in His Sanctuary*, pp. 209, 210). In the heavenly sanctuary, these four likenesses are symbolic of the placement and the qualities of the *cherubim* that surround our Great High Priest. They have the qualities of the lion, the ox, the flying eagle, and the man. They represent God.

The *cherubim* on the ark of the earthly sanctuary have the same attributes of the four "living creatures" in Revelation 4:6–8. As Hardinge said, "Each had the faces of a man, a lion, an ox and an eagle." If we were to diagram these "living creatures" around the throne of God, and put them in the same order that the tribes of Israel were arranged, what would we see?

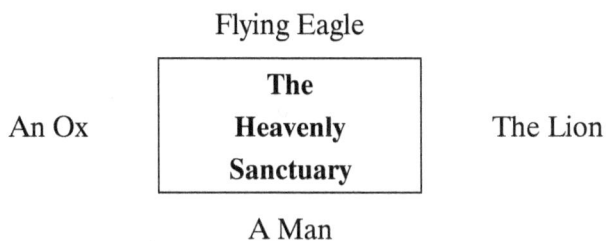

If the earthly sanctuary is a pattern for the heavenly sanctuary, then we may know how the "living creatures" are situated in the heavenly sanctuary. Angels surround the throne of God. They exhibit the character of God, and they are often called *cherubim* in Scripture. Let us explore this term.

Cherubim

Cherubim (the singular is *cherub*) are celestial beings in Scripture who are described in different ways. *Cherubim* first appear as guardians at the Garden of Eden after Adam and Eve were expelled. They later appear in the furnishings of the earthly sanctuary built by Moses. The term *seraphim*, which literally means "burning ones," is another term used in Scripture to describe these special angels who are portrayed as guardians of the throne of God. Qualities of *cherubim* and *seraphim* are described in Isaiah and Ezekiel with fascinating detail. Describing the seraphim Ellen White says, "In bearing His image, in doing His bidding, in worshiping Him, their highest ambition is reached" (*Gospel Workers*, p. 21).

Cherub describes the character of an angel who stands next to the throne of God. Hebrews describes the holy angels as spiritual beings who minister to humanity. "Are they not all ministering spirits sent forth to minister for those who will inherit salvation?" (Heb. 1:14). The physical description of *cherubim* in Scripture tells less about their outer qualities and more about their inner character. *Cherubim* stand next to the throne of God. They are like God.

Isaiah's experience in seeing *cherubim* illustrates their work. What did he see when he was permitted to look upon the Most Holy Place of the heavenly sanctuary? Ellen White explains:

> When God was about to send Isaiah with a message to His people, He first permitted the prophet to look in vision into the holy of holies within the sanctuary. Suddenly the gate and the inner veil of the temple seemed to be uplifted or withdrawn, and he was permitted to gaze within, upon the holy of holies, where even the prophet's feet might not enter. There rose before him a vision of Jehovah sitting upon a throne high and lifted up, while the train of His glory filled the temple. Around the throne were seraphim, as guards about the great King, and they reflected the glory that surrounded them. As their songs of praise resounded in deep notes of adoration, the pillars of the gate trembled, as if shaken by an earthquake. With lips unpolluted by sin, these angels poured forth the praises of God. "Holy, holy, holy, is the Lord of hosts," they cried; "the whole earth is full of His glory."

The seraphim around the throne are so filled with reverential awe as they behold the glory of God, that they do not for an instant look upon themselves with admiration. Their praise is for the Lord of hosts. As they look into the future, when the whole earth shall be filled with His glory, the triumphant song is echoed from one to another in melodious chant, "Holy, holy, holy, is the Lord of hosts." They are fully satisfied to glorify God; abiding in His presence, beneath His smile of approbation, they wish for nothing more. In bearing His image, in doing His bidding, in worshiping Him, their highest ambition is reached.

As the prophet listened, the glory, the power, and the majesty of the Lord was opened to his vision; and in the light of this revelation his own inward defilement appeared with startling clearness. His very words seemed vile to him. In deep humiliation he cried, "Woe is me! for I am undone; because I am a man of unclean lips: . . . for mine eyes have seen the King, the Lord of hosts."

Isaiah's humiliation was genuine. As the contrast between humanity and the divine character was made plain to him, he felt altogether inefficient and unworthy. How could he speak to the people the holy requirements of Jehovah?

"Then flew one of the seraphim unto me," he writes, "having a live coal in his hand, which he had taken with the tongs from off the altar: and he laid it upon my mouth, and said, Lo, this hath touched thy lips; and thine iniquity is taken away, and thy sin purged."

Then Isaiah heard the voice of the Lord, saying, "Whom shall I send, and who will go for us?" and strengthened by the thought of the divine touch, he answered, "Here am I; send me." (*Gospel Workers*, pp. 21, 22)

Before Isaiah was sent on a mission from God, he was given this important vision. He saw the seraphim around the throne of God. They sing, worship, and praise God. The words of their praise sound familiar. "Holy, holy, holy, is the Lord of Host." We read the same chorus in Revelation 4. John tells us: "the four living creatures, each having six wings, were full of eyes around and within. And they do not rest day or night, saying: 'Holy, holy, holy, Lord God Almighty, Who was and is and is to come!' " (Rev. 4:8).

A Former Cherub

Satan was at one time an angel of God. Ezekiel 28:16 describes him as the "covering cherub" who fell from perfection. Ellen White also identifies him as once being "a shining seraph." He once stood next to Jehovah. Ellen White says: "God made him good and beautiful, as near as possible like Himself" (*Review and Herald*, Sept. 21, 1901). The following paragraph is a description of that former cherub and seraph. It helps us to understand how vitally related these beings are to God and His throne.

> As if entranced, the wicked have looked upon the coronation of the Son of God. They see in His hands the tables of the divine law, the statutes which they have despised and transgressed. They witness the outburst of wonder, rapture, and adoration from the saved; and as the wave of melody sweeps over the multitudes without the city, all with one voice exclaim, "Great and marvelous are Thy works, Lord God Almighty; just and true are Thy ways, Thou King of saints" (Revelation 15:3); and, falling

prostrate, they worship the Prince of life.

Satan seems paralyzed as he beholds the glory and majesty of Christ. He who was once a covering cherub remembers whence he has fallen. A shining seraph, "son of the morning;" how changed, how degraded! From the council where once he was honored, he is forever excluded. He sees another now standing near to the Father, veiling His glory. He has seen the crown placed upon the head of Christ by an angel of lofty stature and majestic presence, and he knows that the exalted position of this angel might have been his. (*The Great Controversy*, pp. 668, 669)

Who is it that Satan saw standing near to God the Father? Ellen White identifies the angel in describing his visit with Zacharias prior to the birth of John the Baptist.

To the question of Zacharias, the angel said, "I am Gabriel, that stand in the presence of God; and am sent to speak unto thee, and to show thee these glad tidings." Five hundred years before, Gabriel had made known to Daniel the prophetic period which was to extend to the coming of Christ. The knowledge that the end of this period was near had moved Zacharias to pray for the Messiah's advent. Now the very messenger through whom the prophecy was given had come to announce its fulfillment.

The words of the angel, "I am Gabriel, that stand in the presence of God," show that he holds a position of high honor in the heavenly courts. When he came with a message to Daniel, he said, "There is none that holdeth with me in these things, but Michael [Christ] your Prince." Dan. 10:21. Of Gabriel the Saviour speaks in the Revelation, saying that "He sent and signified it by His angel unto His servant John." Rev. 1:1. And to John the angel declared, "I am a fellow servant with thee and with thy brethren the prophets." Rev. 22:9, R. V. Wonderful thought—that the angel who stands next in honor to the Son of God is the one chosen to open the purposes of God to sinful men. (*The Desire of Ages*, pp. 98, 99)

The Work of the Cherubim

These "living creatures" are *cherubim*, also called *seraphim*, who stand next to the throne of God in the heavenly sanctuary. They are fascinating and powerful celestial beings who are difficult to explain in human terms. Their work in Revelation is to direct John's attention to the throne of God, especially when the seals are being opened. Notice how Revelation 6 describes their work.

Now I saw when the Lamb opened one of the seals: and I heard one of the four living creatures saying with a voice like thunder, "*Come and see* …" When He opened the second seal, I heard the second living creature saying, "*Come and see* …" When He opened the third seal, I heard the third living creature say, "*Come and see* …" When He opened the fourth seal, I heard the voice of the fourth living creature saying, "*Come and see* …" (Rev. 6:1, 3, 5, 7, emphasis added)

Cherubim represent God and point us to the work of God. They are not only guardians of God's throne but direct the work of God—the sending out of messages from the throne room of heaven. Let us line up the four living creatures in Revelation 4 and the work of the four horsemen in Revelation 6. They are connected.

Revelation 4	Revelation 6
First living creature, like a lion	White horse
Second living creature, like a calf	Red horse
Third living creature, like a man's face	Black horse
Four living creature, like a flying eagle	Green/pale horse

There is a celestial order in God's work. The tribes of Israel were placed in a certain way around the sanctuary; the angels of God surround His throne in a certain pattern; and the horses and riders in Revelation 6 come in a certain order. God's government has a method and a plan to teach us something about heavenly things. What order does God give us in the first verse of Revelation?

The Revelation of Jesus Christ, which God gave Him to show His servants—things which must shortly take place. And He sent and signified it by His angel to His servant John. (Rev. 1:1)

This verse can be diagramed as follows:

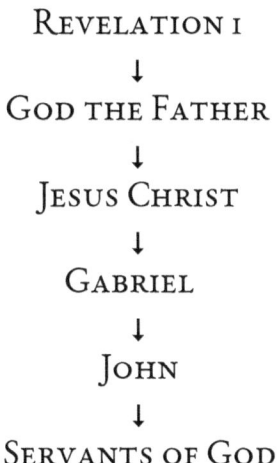

REVELATION 1
↓
GOD THE FATHER
↓
JESUS CHRIST
↓
GABRIEL
↓
JOHN
↓
SERVANTS OF GOD

In this very first verse of Revelation, we see the agents and directional pattern of God's communication with earth. Communication proceeds from the throne of God, where God the Father is seated with Jesus by His side. Then, like ripples from a pebble dropped into a still body of water, it produces waves that flow outwardly from the center, extending to the angels of God, then to the servants of God, like John, and finally to those who follow in Jesus' steps. This is how God communicates what He wants us to know about Himself and about His plans. Notice how this same pattern of celestial order is present in Revelation 6.

REVELATION 6
↓
GOD THE FATHER
↓
JESUS CHRIST
↓
ANGELS OF GOD
↓
FOUR HORSES
↓
RIDERS

We will discuss the correlation of these chains in our next chapter.

Summary

God has a message to communicate with the world. Revelation 1 and 6 reveal that He communicates it is a divine chain of communication that extends from the throne room of heaven to the world. Revelation 1:1 tells us the message is about Jesus Christ, and it says that the message is about things that "must shortly take place." What is this message? The answer comes in Revelation 6 as we give careful study to the four horses and their riders.

Chapter 5

THE MESSAGE OF THE WHITE HORSE: THE GOSPEL RECEIVED?

It has been the dream of many a young maiden. She is in distress and calls for help. Suddenly a dashing young man rides up on a white horse. He quickly strikes down the enemy, then leans over and sweeps her up in his strong arms, setting her on his horse. Together they gallop off into the sunset where they live happily ever after. Never mind that in real life there is more blood and death in battle than unscathed victories.

Some of the greatest paintings regarding battle over the centuries show a general riding a white horse, such as Jean-Baptiste-Édouard Detaille's "Charge of the Fourth Hussars at the battle of Friedland, 14 June 1807," and John Trumbull's famous painting, "The Surrender of Lord Cornwallis at Yorktown, October 19, 1781." In the latter, George Washington parades victoriously between the two armies atop a stately white horse. The famous "Lone Ranger" on film and television rode a white horse named "Silver." Yet, such white horses are very rare. Most white horses are actually gray horses whose coats have turned completely white.

The First Horse

As we begin our study of the first of four horses and horsemen in Revelation 6, we discover a white horse and its rider. What do they symbolize? John writes:

> Now I saw when the Lamb opened one of the seals; and I heard one of the four living creatures saying with a voice like thunder, "Come and see." And I looked, and behold, a white horse. He who sat on it had a bow; and a crown was given to him, and he went out conquering and to conquer. (Rev. 6:1, 2)

John hears one of the living creatures introduce this first horse. Since the other living creatures are identified numerically as the "second," "third," and "fourth," we can assume that the living described as being "like a lion" (Rev. 4:7) is the first. The rider introduced by the first living creature is on a white horse, holding a bow and receiving a crown. The horse and its rider "went out conquering and to conquer" (Rev. 6:2). The scene is one of a battle and victory.

The first living creature is associated with the white horse because it introduces this horse and rider. Remarkably, in the wilderness sanctuary, the symbol on the standard of the tribe of Judah, was a lion. This is also how the first living creature is described. The banner for Judah was placed on the east side of the sanctuary. If we add the white horse to our diagram introduced in chapter 2, showing the order of the

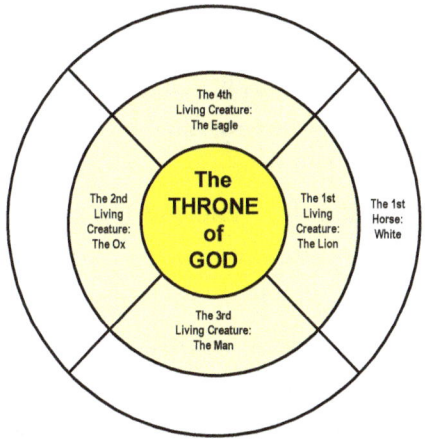

throne room of God and the *cherubim* (the "living creatures"), it might look like the diagram to the right.

A White Horse, a Bow, and a Crown

We have discovered that horses have symbolic meaning in Scripture. The horses in Revelation 6 are swift, powerful and sure-footed animals used in warfare. Why is this horse white? What does the bow and crown represent? And what does it mean that it went out "conquering and to conquer"? We will begin to answer these questions as we consider the meaning of the horse's color, and then consider the symbolism in the description of the rider.

White is the color of purity and spotlessness. Jesus uses this color with His invitation to us: "Though your sins are like scarlet, they shall be white as snow; though they are red like crimson, they shall be as wool" (Isa. 1:18). He declares that those who overcome "shall be clothed in white garments" (Rev. 3:5). These "clean and bright" garments are "the righteousness of the saints" (Rev. 19:8, KJV). White is the color of the character of the saints that overcome through the power of Jesus Christ. It is the message of the good news of the rider on the white horse.

John does not describe the rider on the white horse, but he does say that he had a bow. One of the most effective long-range arms for warfare in Bible times was the bow and arrow. The bow and arrow was widely used by many nations in ancient times and could effectively hit their target from a distance of 300 to 400 yards. Israel had expert archers from the tribe of Benjamin (1 Chron. 8:40). Jehu and Jonathan were both expert marksmen.

Scripture uses the symbol of the arrow many times. Consider the story of King Joash's visit with Elisha when the prophet was on his deathbed. Elisha instructed the king of Israel to take a bow and some arrows and shoot them out a window. What did Elisha say as the arrows flew? "The arrow of the Lord's deliverance ..."

(2 Kings 13:17). The prophet also asked Joash to strike the ground with the arrows. Do you recall Elisha's comment when the king only struck the ground three times? He said: "You should have struck five or six times ... but now you will strike Syria *only* three times" (2 Kings 13:19). The symbolic meaning is clear. God was going to use King Joash to bring deliverance to Israel. Victory came from God through His leaders when He sent them into battle.

Here is another example of arrows representing God's leaders:

> For I have bent Judah, My bow,
> Fitted the bow with Ephraim,
> And raised up your sons, O Zion,
> Against your sons, O Greece,
> And made you like the sword of a mighty man.
> (Zech. 9:13)

God's people are like instruments of war. The Lord uses His servants to conquer the enemy, sending them out, like arrows, to destroy the enemy by His power.

So, what does it mean that the rider of the white horse in Revelation 6 has a bow? Paul tells us that as good soldiers of Christ we should put on the armor of God before each battle with the enemy. He says that we should put on, for protection in the coming battle, the belt of truth, the breastplate of righteousness, the shoes of peace, the shield of faith, and the helmet of salvation (Eph. 6:13–17). The last piece of equipment for the soldier of God is the sword. The sword, Paul writes, is the word of God. Hebrews 4:12 says that the word of God is sharper than any two-edged sword, penetrating to the very thoughts of man. The rider on the white horse carries a bow. As that which he uses to conquer, it is equivalent to the sword, which is the word of God. The gospel of God must be carried to the world. The rider fulfills his responsibility by proclaiming the message of Jesus, which penetrates to the heart of the hearer. It forces them to make a decision—will they choose God and follow Him, or will they choose the mark of the Beast?

Next, notice what is placed on the head of this rider. " ... And a crown was given to him" (Rev. 6:2). What does the crown symbolize in this text? The Greek word for *crown* here is *stephanos* from which we get the name "Stephen." What does the use of the word "crown" represent in this text? *Stephanos* is defined in Vine's *Expository Dictionary of New Testament Words:*

> Crown (στέφανος) [stephanos, Strong's 4735] ... the victor's crown, the symbol of triumph in the games or some such contest; ... a reward or prize ... It was woven as a garland of oak, ivy, parsley, myrtle, or olive, or in imitation of these in gold. In some passages the reference to the games is clear, 1 Cor. 9:25; 2 Tim. 4:8 ("crown of righteousness"); ... In other passages it stands as an emblem of life, joy, reward and glory, Phil. 4:1; 1 Thess. 2:19; Jas 1:12 ("crown of life"); ... It is used of the crown of thorns which the soldiers plaited and put on Christ's head, Matt. 27:29; Mark 15:17; John 19:2, 5. (W. E. Vine, *An Expository Dictionary of New Testament Words*, vol. 1, p. 258)

In order to understand the meaning of this word, we need to consider a few examples of literal crowns in the New Testament. Jesus wore a crown of thorns when He was crucified. "When they had twisted a crown of thorns, they put *it* on His head, and a reed in His right hand" (Matt. 27:29). Paul describes a crown used in athletic contests: "And everyone who competes *for the prize* is temperate in all things. Now they do *it* to obtain a perishable crown ..." (1 Cor. 9:25).

Paul also speaks of symbolic crowns—a "crown of righteousness" (2 Tim. 4:8), a "crown of life" (James 1:12), and a "crown of glory" (1 Peter 5:4). Each instance uses the same Greek word, *stephanos*. Such crowns are the rewards for endurance and pressing forward in the Christian life. They not only describe the character of glory, but also the reward of the saints who are faithful.

Revelation uses this same word eleven times. To the letter to the church of Smyrna, the angel tells John to write, "Be faithful until death, and I will give you the crown [*stephanos*] of life" (Rev. 2:10). To the church of Philadelphia, the angel says, "Hold fast what you have, that no one may take your crown [*stephanos*]" (Rev. 3:11). While the first reference speaks of a future crown, the second reference speaks of a crown that is currently possessed by the holder. When we accept Jesus Christ as our personal Savior, we are given the assurance of salvation, which comes by faith in His righteousness. This "crown of righteousness" does not come by our own works, but by trusting in Jesus.

Another interesting detail in the description of the white horse and rider concerns the direction they are traveling. The rider is not entering heaven, but is sent to the people of the earth. If the rider comes *from* heaven, would he not *represent* heaven? The rider carries a message from the throne room. He represents God's character and work. He is a child of God and goes into battle with a mission from the Father in heaven.

Let us see where each of the four horses and riders is headed. The white horse and rider "went out" (Rev. 6:2) but John does not state where they went. The red horse takes "peace from the earth" (Rev. 6:4). The description of the black horse gives no indication of where it is going. The pale/green horse is given power "over a fourth of the earth" (Rev. 6:8).

Now we can put our findings into a table.

Horse	Description	The Destination
White Horse	Conquering	?
Red Horse	Power to remove peace from the Earth	The Earth
Black Horse	Pair of Balances	?
Pale Horse	Power to destroy the Earth	The Earth

Two of the four riders are carried to destinations on the earth. John does not say where the other two riders are headed. By using our chart, which illustrates the movement of God's message from His throne room out to the four corners of the earth, we can assume that the horses and their riders have a worldwide message. Just as the *cherubim* surround the throne and the standards are planted around the sanctuary, so does the message of God spread north, south, east and west.

Who Are the Riders?

Who are the four riders on these horses? Is the rider on the white horse Jesus Christ? Revelation 19:11–16 does describe Christ riding on a white horse. Nevertheless, when Jesus ascended to heaven, He commanded His disciples: "Go into all the world and preach the gospel to every creature" (Mark 16:15). Christ returned to heaven and entered the sanctuary to begin His priestly work on our behalf. The Lord promised that the Holy Spirit would be poured out to help spread the gospel. Yet, Jesus did not return from heaven to do the work of spreading the gospel. He commissioned His followers to fulfill that task.

Isaiah's experience in beholding God in the sanctuary helps us understand the riders on the horses. When Isaiah saw the Lord in vision (Isa. 6:1), when he saw the seraphim and heard them exclaim, "Holy, holy, holy," and when he experienced the forgiveness of his sins after the angel touched his lips with a coal from the altar, he responded to. God's question, "Whom shall I send, and who will go for Us?" "Here am I! Send me" (Isa. 6:8).

Isaiah was a child of God who recognized his own sinfulness when he said, "Woe is me, for I am undone! because I *am* a man of unclean lips. ..." (Isa. 6:5). Yet, the Lord used Isaiah. James tells us "Elijah was a man with a nature like ours ..." (James 5:17), and he then describes how God used him in a mighty way. When Paul and Barnabas, through the power of God, healed a man in Lystra, the people thought they were gods. Paul and Barnabas set the record straight, saying, "Men, why are you doing these things? We also are men with the same nature as you ..." (Acts 14:15).

Whom does God send as messengers from the throne room of heaven into all the world? Who rides forth with the confidence and power of heaven, with the arrows of truth and the assurance of salvation? God sends His disciples. If you are a follower of Jesus, you are like one riding a white horse with a message to take to the world. You enter a battlefield with strength in your hand and victory on your head. You are not alone. Christ's presence, through the Holy Spirit, is always near. The bow and crown remind us of the power that comes from God. What an awesome responsibility!

We find another indicator that we are like horsemen carrying a message to the world in the pattern in the chain of communication found in the first verse of Revelation. The pattern emanates from God's heavenly throne room. Notice the flow and order of the message: "The Revelation of Jesus Christ, which God gave Him to show His servants—things which must shortly take place And He sent and signified it by His angel to His servant John" (Rev. 1:1). Who are the links in the chain?

- *God* gave *Jesus* a message
- Jesus gave *Gabriel* the message
- Gabriel gave *John* the message
- John gave *the servants of Jesus* the message

Who is missing from this chain of communication if we compare it to Revelation 6? It would be the horses and riders. Yet, they find their place when we diagram them as follows:

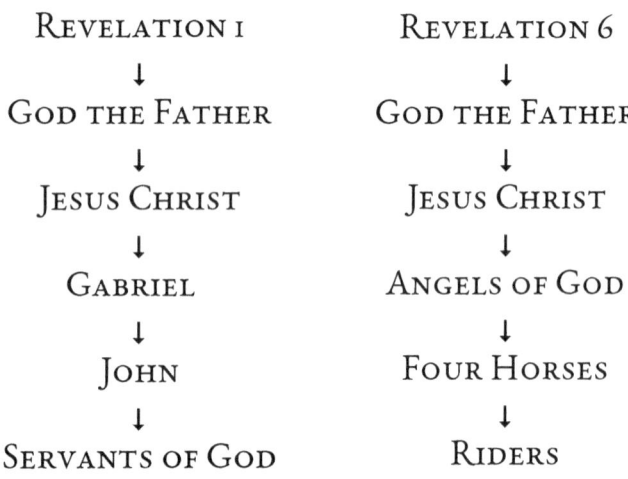

The book of Revelation contains a message that God wants carried to the world. Through Jesus Christ and His angelic messengers, God gave John a great prophecy. This message of "things which must shortly take place" was not meant for himself. The prophecies of Revelation are to be taken by God's servants to the world. The correlation of the patterns of communication in Revelation 1 and 6 shows us that the riders are God's servants, people like you and me! We are to go into all the world.

The White Horse Message

What message is represented by the white horse and rider? What is to be communicated to the four corners of the earth? What is the work of the rider? Revelation says, "… he went out conquering and to conquer" (Rev. 6:2). What does that mean? If conquering equates with battle, what is the war? Notice how Ellen White describes our work at the end of time. Several times she uses the phrase from the description of the white horse and rider, "conquering and to conquer." All of these are in the context of our work as servants of Christ, following our Leader.

> Impelled and stimulated by the love of Christ, as God's people advance in the work marked out for them, they will conquer through faith. By faith they may behold even more than angels in their ranks; for the abundant aid of the General of armies is ready for them in every emergency. He leads them on from victory to victory, proclaiming at every step, "I have overcome the world." Your leader goeth forth, *conquering and to conquer*. Never forget that you are fighting the battle of the Lord of hosts, in full view of the invisible world. (*Review and Herald*, March 15, 1898, emphasis supplied)

We conquer through faith. We are moved by our love for Christ. We believe that angels work beside us and Christ leads before us. We are fighting the battle of the Lord of hosts and Christ, our General, has already overcome the world. How will we, His army, overcome? Christ sought to point His disciples toward victory during His last moments with them in the upper room before His trial and crucifixion. He did not tell of His sufferings but pointed them to the truth by which they would overcome.

> He rejoiced in the consciousness that He could and would do more for His followers than He had promised; that from Him would flow forth love and compassion, cleansing the soul temple, and making men like Him in character; that His truth, armed with the power of the Spirit, would go forth *conquering and to conquer*. (*The Acts of the Apostles*, p. 23, emphasis supplied)

Our battle is to spread the truth about God through the gospel of Jesus Christ. The enemy has spread lies about the Father, and it is our privilege to bring the truth about sin and salvation, about God's love for fallen mankind to the world. Jesus has sent His brothers and sisters out in the world that they might stay the tide of moral evil.

> God's workers must gain a far deeper experience. If they will surrender all to Him, He will work mightily for them. They will plant the standard of truth upon fortresses till then held by Satan, and with shouts of victory take possession of them. They bear the scars of battle, but there comes to them the comforting message that the Lord will lead them on, *conquering and to conquer.* (*Colporteur Ministry*, p. 155, emphasis supplied)

Whom will God send to spread this message to the world? Like Isaiah, we should be quick to say, "Here *am* I! Send me" (Isa. 6:8) Like those who have gone before us—Abraham, Moses, Daniel, John and others—we can go forth conquering in the power of God. If you are in doubt, remember what the Bible says: "I can do all things through Christ who strengthens me ... And my God shall supply all your need according to His riches in glory by Christ Jesus" (Phil. 4:13, 19).

What does the rider have besides the bow and the crown? Ellen White answers:

> Clad in the armor of Christ's righteousness, the church is to enter upon her final conflict. "Fair as the moon, clear as the sun, and terrible as an army with banners" (Song of Solomon 6:10), she is to go forth into all the world, conquering and to conquer. (*Prophets and Kings*, p. 725)

What does this battle look like? Ellen White declares:

> In vision I saw two armies in terrible conflict. One army was led by banners bearing the world's insignia; the other was led by the bloodstained banner of Prince Immanuel. Standard after standard was left to trail in the dust as company after company from the Lord's army joined the foe and tribe after tribe from the ranks of the enemy united with the commandment-keeping people of God. An angel flying in the midst of heaven put the standard of Immanuel into many hands, while a mighty general cried out with a loud voice: "Come into line. Let those who are loyal to the commandments of God and the testimony of Christ now take their position. Come out from among them, and be ye separate, and touch not the unclean, and I will receive you, and will be a Father unto you, and ye shall be My sons and daughters. Let all who will come up to the help of the Lord, to the help of the Lord against the mighty."
>
> The battle raged. Victory alternated from side to side. Now the soldiers of the cross gave way, "as when a standardbearer fainteth." Isaiah 10:18. But their apparent retreat was but to gain a more advantageous position. Shouts of joy were heard. A song of praise to God went up, and angel voices united in the song, as Christ's soldiers planted His banner on the walls of fortresses till then held by the enemy. The Captain of our salvation was ordering the battle and sending support to His soldiers. His power was mightily displayed, encouraging them to press the battle to the gates. He taught them terrible things in

righteousness as He led them on step by step, conquering and to conquer.

At last the victory was gained. The army following the banner with the inscription, "The commandments of God, and the faith of Jesus," was gloriously triumphant. The soldiers of Christ were close beside the gates of the city, and with joy the city received her King. The kingdom of peace and joy and everlasting righteousness was established. (*Testimonies for the Church*, vol. 8, p. 41)

Two thousand years ago the disciples of Jesus Christ carried this message to the uttermost parts of the earth. Once again, God's people are commissioned to carry the message of the three angels, as the riders on the four horses carry their message, to the uttermost parts of the inhabited earth. When will this happen? At the time of the end, which is now. We are now living at that time.

Summary

We are now entering into the final battle of the Lord of Hosts. The truth of the everlasting gospel is to be carried to the four corners of the world, that every human being might make the choice between good and evil. God is asking His children to represent Him in this final conflict with the forces of evil. He has given His children training in righteousness. He promises to provide the means to get them to the four corners of the earth. He promises to place in their hands the greatest weapon in the universe. He promises them victory. The message of the white horse is clear. We are to go forth conquering in the name of Jesus and by His righteousness and power. Each of us, like Isaiah, may look into the throne room of heaven and see the work of Christ. And when God's glory comes over us and asks, "Whom shall I send? And who will go for Us?" you and I may quickly say, *Here am I! Send me.*

Chapter 6

THE MESSAGE OF THE RED HORSE: PEACE OR FEAR?

Does a knife wound or heal? It depends. Does a rope save or destroy? It depends. Does water bring life or death? It also depends. How something is received can make a huge difference in the impact of that thing. Alcohol is not evil of itself; it can be used in a way to destroy a person's life, as in alcoholism, or it can be used to save lives, as with an anesthetic. If you leave a candle out in the hot sun, it will melt. However, if you set a piece of clay out in the hot sun, it becomes very hard. Though the sun has not changed, the objects respond to the sun in different ways.

In this chapter we will look at the message of the rider on the red horse. He is given a great sword and power to take peace from the earth. Why would a messenger from heaven "take peace" from the earth? Does God not want to bring peace to the earth? Does the gospel not bring peace? It depends, as we shall see as we dig into the message of the red horse.

The Red Horse

> When He opened the second seal, I heard the second living creature saying, 'Come and see.' Another horse, fiery red, went out. And it was granted to the

one who sat on it to take peace from the earth, and that people should kill one another; and there was given to him a great sword. (Rev. 6:3, 4)

The second living creature says to John, "Come and see." This is the creature with a face like a calf. He calls John's attention to a red horse galloping from the throne of God. Where does the red horse come from? What do the horse and rider represent? If the symbol of a calf, or ox, in the wilderness sanctuary was placed on the west side, by the tribe of Ephraim, then the red horse "went out" from the west side of God's throne. Placing it on the diagram we are building, it would look like this:

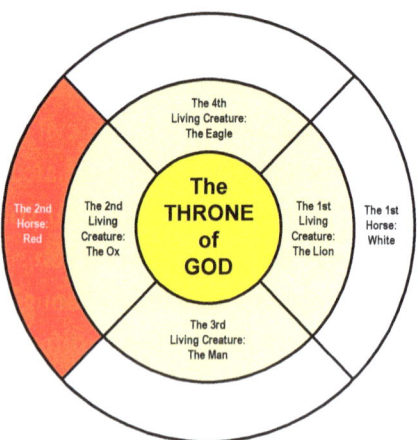

Take Peace from the Earth

What does it mean that this rider was given power to "take peace from the earth"? Let us begin by looking at some examples in the Bible that describe God's giving peace. When Mary Magdalene anointed Jesus with perfume, Christ not only forgave her sins but also said, "Your faith has saved you. Go in peace" (Luke 7:50). On the last night Jesus spent with His disciples, He left these encouraging words: "Peace I leave with you, My peace I give to you; not as the world gives do I give to you. Let not your heart be troubled, neither let it be afraid" (John 14:27). In speaking about salvation, Paul writes, "Therefore, having been justified by faith, we have peace with God through our Lord Jesus Christ" (Rom. 5:1). When we surrender our lives to God and ask Him to wash away our sins, He fills our heart with heaven's peace. As John 14:27 tells us, Christ takes away our fear and gives us peace.

There is another reference to peace, which Jesus makes, that sounds contradictory to these passages. In the context of Christ's sending out the twelve disciples in ministry, Jesus said, "Do not think that I came to bring peace on earth. I did not come to bring peace but a sword" (Matt. 10:34). Is Jesus contradicting Himself? Did Christ not say that He came to bring peace? How are peace and a sword related to one another? If Jesus came to bring peace, then how could He say that He does not bring peace but a sword?

Perhaps what Jesus brings to the earth is one thing—the gospel of salvation—while people's response to the gospel is something else. Notice how Ellen White explains Matthew 10:34:

> Though he bore the title of Prince of Peace, Christ said of himself, "Think not that I am come to send a peace on earth; I came not to send peace, but a sword." By these words he did not mean that his coming was to produce discord and contention among his followers. He desired to show the effect his teaching would have on different minds. One portion of the human family would receive him; the other portion would take sides with Satan, and would oppose Christ and all his followers. The Prince of Peace, he was yet the cause of division. He who came to proclaim glad tidings and create hope and joy in the hearts of the children of men, opened a controversy that burns deep, and arouses intense passion in the human heart. And he warned his

> followers: "In the world ye shall have tribulation." "They shall lay their hands on you, and persecute you, delivering you up to the synagogues, and into prisons, being brought before kings and rulers for my name's sake.... Ye shall be betrayed both by parents and brethren, and kinsfolks, and friends; and some of you shall they cause to be put to death." (*Review and Herald*, Jan. 16, 1900)

The effect of Jesus' teaching is not always the same. Different minds and hearts receive the message in different ways. If you receive the good news of salvation and join yourself to Jesus, you will receive peace. But if you side with Satan and reject the gospel, the message will be like a sword that destroys. Not only that, but those who oppose the message of salvation will seek to take the sword, which brings conviction and turn it against God's people!

Why is the gospel like a sword for some people? Listen to Ellen White's explanation:

> The gospel is a message of peace. Christianity is a system which, received and obeyed, would spread peace, harmony, and happiness throughout the earth. The religion of Christ will unite in close brotherhood all who accept its teachings. It was the mission of Jesus to reconcile men to God, and thus to one another. But the world at large are under the control of Satan, Christ's bitterest foe. The gospel presents to them principles of life which are wholly at variance with their habits and desires, and they rise in rebellion against it. They hate the purity which reveals and condemns their sins, and they persecute and destroy those who would urge upon them its just and holy claims. It is in this

sense—because the exalted truths it brings occasion hatred and strife—that the gospel is called a sword. (*The Great Controversy*, p. 46)

The gospel of Jesus Christ is unchangeable, yet it can bring peace or it can act as a sword. It all depends on the response of the hearer to the message. Love and peace are the prevailing principles of heaven. But when we are confronted with the gospel of Jesus Christ, those who resist the sword that cuts to our hearts to remove sin will rise up in rebellion.

Selfish hearts do not want to submit to the gospel. Even when the gentle voice of Jesus calls like a shepherd to people's hearts, they each have the freedom to turn away. Receiving heaven's peace means a person must give up one's own will and ways. Some may think that they will submit some day, but with every turn toward false teachings, with every sip of the *wine of Babylon* (Rev. 14:8; 18:3), they become more confused and more resistant to Jesus' call. A rebellious spirit grows, and the pure message and the messengers who bring it become the target of their hatred, and to destroy both becomes their way to maintain control. All this strife began when they rejected the invitation to accept the gospel of peace.

Jesus, the Prince of Peace, preached the gospel. He brought the good news to God's people, yet He was looked upon as the enemy of Israel. Ellen White writes:

> His coming must be as the unsheathing of a sword. The kingdom He had come to establish was the opposite of that which the Jews desired. He who was the foundation of the ritual and economy of Israel would be looked upon as its enemy and destroyer. He who had proclaimed the law upon Sinai would be condemned as a transgressor. He who had come

to break the power of Satan would be denounced as Beelzebub ... (*The Desire of Ages*, p. 111)

Truth vs. Lies

How true are the words we just read. Consider the contrast between "the truth" about Jesus and "the lies" about Jesus.

The Truth About Jesus	The Lies About Jesus
He is the foundation and Creator of Israel.	He was called the enemy and destroyer of Israel.
He proclaimed the law on Sinai.	He was condemned as a transgressor of the Law.
He came to break the power of Satan.	He was called Beelzebub, the king of devils.

Christ "desired to show the effect his teaching would have on different minds. One portion of the human family would receive him; the other portion would take sides with Satan, and would oppose Christ and all his followers ..." (*Review and Herald*, January 16, 1900). Not only did the Jewish leaders rise in rebellion to the law of heaven, they opposed Christ who gave them the law, they made up lies about Him, and finally crucified Him. When God's messengers preach the gospel, men will react: some will follow and some will not.

> Men professing the name of Christ have worked against His cause, and the blessing brought to men at infinite cost has been turned into a curse; for when truth is rejected because it is out of harmony

with the corruption of the natural heart, it becomes a sword to destroy. The truth, which was to restore and renew, is a destroyer of evil; and when evil is persistently cherished, it becomes a destroyer of the sinner also.

Strife and opposition have been the sure result of resistance on the part of men, incited by evil angels, to God's plan of mercy. Man's perversity, his resistance of the truth, makes the mission of Christ appear to be what He announced to His disciples,—the sending of a sword upon the earth; but the strife is not the effect of Christianity, but the result of opposition in the hearts of those who will not receive its blessings. (*Bible Echo*, March 12, 1894)

The basic message of the red horse and its rider is no different from that of the white horse. Christ came to bring victory (by the white horse) and peace (by the red horse). Like the seeds in the Parable of the Sower, the message does not change. It is the response of each heart that changes. People respond to the gospel in different ways. We see in the illustration of the red horse and its rider that, though the Prince of Peace came to bring peace to the earth, for those who resist, He becomes like a sword. Strife rises up in the hearts of those who resist the gospel message. The red horse does not seek to take peace from the earth; it is the result of the hearts of the people, who are resistant to the good news of salvation.

Killing One Another

What does the passage mean when it says, " …and that *people* should kill one another …" (Rev 6:4)? How does this fit with the message of the red horse and the removal of peace from the earth? If we look back into the history of Israel, we find a story that is enlightening on this point. It is that of Gideon and his small army coming down upon the Midianites. Here is how Ellen White describes how the enemies of God turn against one another:

> The sleeping army was suddenly aroused. Upon every side was seen the light of the flaming torches. In every direction was heard the sound of trumpets, with the cry of the assailants. Believing themselves at the mercy of an overwhelming force, the Midianites were panic-stricken. With wild cries of alarm they fled for life, and, mistaking their own companions for enemies, they slew one another. As news of the victory spread, thousands of the men of Israel who had been dismissed to their homes returned and joined in pursuit of their fleeing enemies … (*Patriarchs and Prophets*, p. 550)

The Midianites were sleeping when they were suddenly aroused by the noise of the trumpets. When they heard the sound and, when they saw the lights of the flaming torches coming from every direction, they jumped out of their beds and thought that they were at the mercy of an overwhelming force. They were unprepared. Terror struck their hearts; peace turned into fear. They panicked and fled for their lives. In the darkness and confusion, they mistakenly killed one another, illustrating how enemies will turn against one another under the message of the red horse.

Having Christ Brings Peace

There is a simple principle in Scripture that we can trust: When we have Christ in our hearts, we will have peace. On the other hand, when we do not have Christ in our hearts, we will have fear. Paul brings this out when he describes the battle in the heart of every human. He says, "For to be carnally minded is death, but to be spiritually minded is life and peace" (Rom. 8:6). There are only two choices. There are only two pathways we can take. To be carnally minded means to reject Christ, but to be spiritually minded means to accept the Holy Spirit into the heart. When we accept Christ we will have peace.

John writes in his Gospel about different reactions to the message of salvation. In describing Jesus as the light of the world, he says, "... everyone practicing evil hates the light and does not come to the light, lest his deeds should be exposed. But he who does the truth comes to the light, that his deeds may be clearly seen, that they have been done in God" (John 3:20, 21).

Fear is the opposite of peace. The "spirit of fear" undermines peace. On the other hand, several Bible writers describe the overcoming of fear. Paul says, "For you did not receive the spirit of bondage again to fear, but you received the Spirit of adoption by whom we cry out, 'Abba, Father' (Rom. 8:15). He reminds Timothy, "For God has not given us a spirit of fear, but of power and of love and of a sound mind" (2 Tim. 1:7). John writes in his first epistle to the churches, "There is no fear in love; but perfect love casts out fear, because fear involves torment. But he who fears has not been made perfect in love" (1 John 4:18).

Summary

The red horse and its rider leave God's throne room in heaven and go out into the world to spread a message. One result is that peace is taken from the earth. Though the message is meant to bring peace, people who resist the gospel find themselves living in fear and turning on others as they turn away from God. These not only seek to destroy the messengers of God, but they even slaughter one another, as happened during the time of Gideon.

Ellen White writes about this difficult time in one of her earliest compositions:

> About four months since, I had a vision of events, all in the future. And I saw the time of trouble, such as never was,—Jesus told me it was the time of Jacob's trouble, and that we should be delivered out of it by the voice of God. Just before we entered it, we all received the seal of the living God. Then I saw the four Angels cease to hold the four winds. And I saw famine, pestilence and sword, nation rose against nation, and the whole world was in confusion ... (Ellen G. Harmon, *The Day-Star*, March 14, 1846)

When God's presence is finally removed from the earth, there will be great confusion. The rejection of the gospel is like the rider on the red horse who brings a sword to the world. Fear and turmoil turn people against God's people and against each other. We have a choice. We can turn to Christ and live, or we can turn away from the gospel, live in fear, and die. It is a simple but important choice we must all make.

Chapter 7

The Message of the Black Horse: Freedom or Slavery?

How much would you pay for a loaf of bread? Harrods, London's premier department store, is selling a luxurious loaf of bread. It is Britain's most expensive bread—the Roquefort and Almond sourdough. Paul Hollywood, the master baker who makes it, calls it the "Rolls-Royce of loafs." It is made from "Grade A" flour from a specialist miller from France, and it contains no additives or preservatives. Currently, it sells for about $24.50 a loaf.

Revelation 6 also describes a black horse and its rider, which symbolically announce that there is coming a time when a plain loaf of bread will sell for a similar inflated price. Yet, the circumstances are not holiday festivities among the rich. Rather, they will be the result of famine. Yet, is the passage describing hunger for bread or for something more? We will see as we examine the message of the third horse and horseman.

The Black Horse

> When He opened the third seal, I heard the third living creature say, "Come and see." So I looked, and behold, a black horse, and he who sat on it had a

pair of scales in his hand. And I heard a voice in the midst of the four living creatures saying, "A quart of wheat for a denarius, and three quarts of barley for a denarius; and do not harm the oil and the wine." (Rev. 6:5, 6)

The third living creature, the creature with a "face like a man" (Rev. 4:7), introduces the third horse and rider. John once more is invited to "come and see." This rider is carrying a pair of scales in his hand. As John recounts his vision, he hears a voice from among the four living creatures, talking about wheat, barley, oil, wine, and the denarius. What does this black horse, galloping away from the throne of God mean? According to our diagram, the horse is traveling to the south.

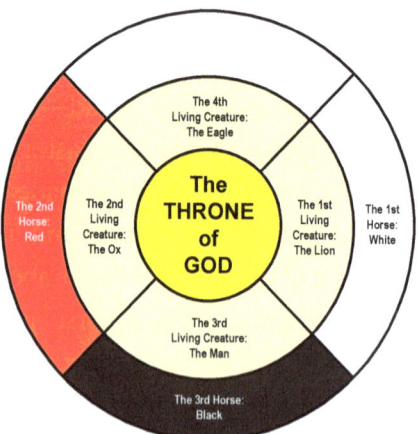

On the standard of the tribe of Reuben in the wilderness sanctuary was the face of a man. The tribe of Reuben was located to the south of the sanctuary. Since the third living creature has the face of a man and was introduced by the third living creature, we can place the third horse to the south of the throne.

A Pair of Balances

Why does the rider of the black horse have a pair of balances in his hand? What does this represent? If the message of the first two horses is the same—the gospel—but the response to the gospel varies, then what is the effect of the black horse, whose rider holds a pair of balances in his hand? Let us look more closely at the original word used for "scales" in this passage.

The Greek word for "balances," which can be identified by using *Strong's Exhaustive Concordance,* is *zugŏs* (Strong's 2218). It is defined as, "from the root of *zĕugnumi* (to *join,* espec. by a "yoke"); a *coupling,* i.e. (fig.) *servitude* (a *law* or *obligation*); also (lit.) the *beam* of the balance (as *connecting* the scales):—pair of balances, yoke." The word *zugŏs* is translated "yoke" five times in the New Testament and only once as "a pair of balances." The root word emphasizes "joining" or "coupling" two things together.

Let us look at some examples of *zugŏs* in the New Testament, using the same word as found in Revelation 6:5. When Paul encourages bondservants to honor their masters, he speaks of them being "under the yoke" (1 Tim. 6:1). At the Jerusalem council, Peter spoke against the Gentiles needing circumcision. Upholding salvation by grace through faith, he said to the group, "Now therefore, why do you test God by putting a yoke on the neck of the disciples which neither our fathers nor we were able to bear?" (Acts 15:10). Along the same lines, Paul counseled the church in Galatia, which was being influenced by Judaizers: "Stand fast therefore in the liberty by which Christ has made us free, and do not be entangled again with a yoke of bondage" (Gal. 5:1).

Perhaps the best-known use of *zugŏs* comes from the words of Jesus when He spoke to the people about being burdened by the teachings of the Pharisees. Matthew records His words: "Come to Me, all *you* who labor and are heavy laden, and I will give you rest. Take My yoke upon you and learn from Me, for I am gentle and lowly in heart, and you will find rest for your souls. For My yoke is easy and My burden is light" (Matt. 11:28–30).

These examples of *zugŏs* help us understand that there is a yoke that can weigh people down, that can bind them to slavery and keep them from being free. How might these examples help us understand the use of this word in Revelation 6:5? Though almost all translations use the words "pair of scales," or "pair of balances," to translate the term, perhaps John intended a deeper meaning for *zugŏs*, in keeping with the way it is used throughout the rest of the New Testament. Maybe the rider of the black horse was actually holding up a *yoke* to teach us a spiritual truth. What would the symbol in Revelation mean if this were the case?

Let us look again at Jesus' words in Matthew 11:28–30. There He taught that we should take "His yoke" on ourselves. That is, He invites us to be joined to Him. Yokes were wooden crossbeams used to link two animals together, such as when oxen are joined to pull a plow. Christians are not to carry wooden beams around their necks; they are not to be joined to cattle. What Jesus wants is that we follow His teachings and walk with Him on the path of life.

Ellen White speaks to those who are aching under heavy loads of care, who try to live up to the standards of the world. Living for the world wears people out. She says: "Our Lord desires them to lay aside this yoke of bondage. He invites them to accept His yoke; He says, 'My yoke is easy, and My burden is light' (*Desire of Ages*, p. 330). The ways of mankind create worry and wound the consciences of people. Worry is a yoke of bondage. The burden of guilt is a yoke of bondage. As we walk with Christ in His yoke, these perplexities vanish and our burden of guilt is taken away. Our pathway is lightened by Jesus' presence.

Commenting further on this passage, Mrs. White says:

> In these words Christ is speaking to every human being. Whether they know it or not, all are weary and heavy-laden. All are weighed down with burdens that only Christ can remove. The heaviest burden

> that we bear is the burden of sin. If we were left to bear this burden, it would crush us. But the Sinless One has taken our place. "The Lord hath laid on Him the iniquity of us all." Isa. 53:6. He has borne the burden of our guilt. He will take the load from our weary shoulders. He will give us rest. The burden of care and sorrow also He will bear. He invites us to cast all our care upon Him; for He carries us upon His heart. (*The Desire of Ages*, p. 328)

Sin is the greatest burden we can bear. Christ lifts the yoke of sin. He removes this weight and gives us rest. We may place all our burdens on Him. Mrs. White explains the purpose of a yoke:

> The yoke is an instrument of service. Cattle are yoked for labor, and the yoke is essential that they may labor effectually. By this illustration Christ teaches us that we are called to service as long as life shall last. We are to take upon us His yoke, that we may be co-workers with Him. (*The Desire of Ages*, p. 329)

Oxen are brought together for labor by the use of a yoke, which makes their work more efficient. The yoke symbolizes our willing connection to Christ for God's service. The connection is driven by love and will be the controlling power in our lives. "For we are God's fellow workers" (1 Cor. 3:9). We will experience the principle of co-operative service with God as Jesus will be at our side in every trial, in every work, in every word, and in every thought. Those with whom we come in contact will recognize that we have been with Him.

Burdens are unavoidable. They come to us all. We experience them every day. Yet, Christ would have our burdens to be light by our living in connection with Him. We do not need to carry the burden of sin. The trials that come our way need not weigh us down when we walk with Jesus linked beside us. The righteous life of Christ becomes our life. His yoke frees us from the yoke of bondage and of sin. To turn down the wooden yoke of Christ, Ellen White tells us, means settling for a "yoke of iron" (*Testimonies for the Church*, vol. 4, 172).

In Paul's words to the Galatians, he warns us not to be entangled by the yoke of bondage. We can think of Paul's saying, "Christ has made us free" (Gal. 5:1), in terms of the yoke of Christ, which is the yoke of His righteousness. It is our choice which yoke we will wear.

The greatest battle that has ever been fought—or that ever will be fought—is the battle against self (*Steps to Christ*, p. 43). Though God offers mankind salvation through His infinite love and power, only a few choose to "come to Him that they might have life" (*The Great Controversy*, p. 22). This rider is holding up the *zugŏs*. It is as if he is holding up a choice. Joshua appeals to the people: "choose for yourselves this day whom you will serve" (Josh. 24:15). That is the rider's basic question: Which side will you choose? Which yoke will you wear? Which way will the balance of the scale fall? Will you choose freedom, or will you choose slavery? The Book of Revelation has given us a view that affects all mankind, and all mankind need to know the choice they must make. Very soon those who refuse the invitation of Jesus will stand in judgment before the King of the Universe.

"A Quart of Wheat for a Denarius"

Let us continue with the rest of the passage on the black horse. Notice the second part of the message— "And I heard a voice in the midst of the four living creatures saying, 'A quart of wheat for a denarius, and three quarts of barley for a denarius; and do not harm the oil and the wine'" (Rev. 6:6). What is the meaning of "a quart of wheat"?

The Greek word for "quart" in this passage is *choinix*. It is translated "measure" in the King James Version. *Vine's Expository*

Dictionary says that *choinix*, "a dry measure of rather less than a quart, about 'as much as would support a person of moderate appetite for a day,' occurs in Revelation 6:6 (twice). Usually eight *chœnixes* could be bought for a *denarius* (about 9½ d.) ..." (*An Expository Dictionary of New Testament Words*, vol. 2, pp. 52, 53). Thus, the passage is a prediction of famine in which a single *choinix* of wheat sells for a denarius.

What is a denarius? The King James Version translates *denarius* as "penny," which was a day's wages. Regarding a "day's wages," the *Bible Knowledge Commentary* says:

> *A day's wages* refers to a silver coin, the Roman denarius, worth about 15 cents, which was the normal wage for a worker for an entire day. So this passage is saying that in that food shortage an entire day's work would be required to buy either a quart of wheat or three quarts of barley. If one bought wheat, it would be enough for one good meal; if he bought barley, it would be enough for three good meals but nothing would be left for buying oil or wine. Famine is the inevitable aftermath of war. ... (*Bible Knowledge Commentary*, p. 948)

Commenting on this same passage, the *InterVarsity Press Bible Background Commentary of The New Testament* says:

> Barley and wheat were basic staples. Because a quart of wheat was a day's sustenance, and a denarius was a day's wage, a man with a family would have to buy the cheaper barley instead. Even then, three quarts of barley was hardly enough daily food for a whole family to subsist on; in the many peasant families with large numbers of children, several children

would die. The famine also created a high inflation rate: this wheat costs more than ten times the average price of wheat.

Oil and wine were widely used, but not essential like wheat or barley. Oil was especially used for anointing the head, washing the body and lighting lamps; wine was mixed with water (one part wine for two to three parts water) for meals. The selective continuance of such items of relatively secondary importance while staples were barely obtainable would reinforce the reality of divine judgment (Craig S. Keener, *The InterVarsity Press Bible Background Commentary New Testament*, p. 780.

Let us translate this into today's terms. If the basic wage was equal to today's minimum wage of about $7.25 per hour and the workday is eight hours long, what would be your basic wage each working day? Eight hours times $7.25 per hour equals $58.00.

According to Revelation 6:6, with 58 dollars—a day's wage—a person could buy just one quart of wheat. One quart of wheat makes about two loaves of bread. So, two loaves of wheat bread at the cheapest cost would be $58. That is a lot of money! Is bread worth $29.00 per loaf? It is if you are really hungry! Why does the message of the black horse speak of buying so little bread for so much money?

Could the warning of the rider of the black horse be that, with the false doctrines and bondage of Babylon, comes famine? Yet, it is not just a famine of food but worse, of the words of the Lord. As Amos declared, "'Behold, the days are coming,' says the Lord God, 'That I will send a famine on the land, not a famine of bread, nor a thirst for water, but of hearing the words of the Lord'" (Amos 8:11). If the people of the world are not eating the word of God, they will starve to death. They will not have the words of

God unless we bring them. When God calls for riders, we must answer, "Send me."

We must get ready for the coming crisis. We must memorize God's word. We must prepare for this final attack of Satan. If the famine is spiritual, this would mean that the rider is offering the bread of life to a starving world. All must know and answer the question: *Will you turn to the bread of life and live?*

Chapter 8

THE MESSAGE OF THE GREEN HORSE: LIFE OR DEATH?

Imagine you hired a neighbor boy to care for your yard while you are away on a three-month trip. It is summertime so you carefully instruct him on watering and mowing. While you are gone, you call the boy and ask, "How do things look?" He hesitates, so you press, "Is the grass *green*?" He finally mumbles, "Sort of." When you return from your trip and pull into your driveway you discover the grass is pale-yellow with barely a touch of green. You learn the boy never watered your lawn once. Would you pay the boy? Probably not. Your lawn is basically dead. It will take a near miracle for it to be green again anytime soon.

The problem was not with the grass. There was nothing wrong with the lawn. The same lawn looked beautiful before you left. The problem was in the boy. He chose not to water the lawn and it died. That is a bit like the message of the fourth horseman in Revelation 6 that we will be looking at in this chapter. When we read about this horse and rider, ask yourself: *Is the problem with the message or with the message's reception?*

The Fourth Horse

When He opened the fourth seal, I heard the voice

The Message of the Green Horse: Life or Death? 97

of the fourth living creature say, 'Come and see.' So I looked, and behold a pale horse. And the name of him who sat on it was Death, and Hades followed with him. And power was given to them over a fourth of the earth, to kill with sword, with hunger, with death, and by the beasts of the earth. (Rev. 6:7, 8)

Here we see the last of the four horses of the Apocalypse. The appearance of the horse is somewhat startling. The rider is Death; the horse is "pale" (or perhaps green) and its rider is given power to kill. A pale horse sounds like a sick horse. The companion of the rider called Death is Hell. That is a fateful twin. This truly gives a gloomy foreboding of what will someday happen to mankind on the earth.

The fourth living creature, with the face of a flying eagle, introduces this horse and rider. The horse gallops from God's throne. If the standard of an eagle in the wilderness sanctuary belongs to the tribe of Dan, it would be located to the north. Let us add this horse to our diagram.

Before we consider the message of this pale horse and its rider, let us review a few things we have already learned while studying this vision of John in Revelation 6. First, we learned that these four horses come from the throne of God and go out into all the earth. Next, we determined that the basic message of salvation is given by all the riders, regardless of the color of their horse. Yet, the color of the horse and the distinctions of what their riders are carrying highlight the way that different minds receive or reject the message. Humans do not all respond to God's final message in the same way.

Pale or Green?

So, what is the purpose of the pale horse with a rider named Death and a partner named *Hell?* Let us begin with the color of the horse. The King James Version describes the horse's color as "pale." The Greek word for "pale" in this verse is *chloros* (Strong's 5515). *Strong's Exhaustive Concordance* provides the definition:

> *Chlōroŏs:* from the same as *5514; greenish*, i.e. *verdant*, *dun-colored:*—green, pale." For 5514, Strong's says: "*Chlŏē, khlŏ'-ay;* fem. of appar. a prim. word; "*green*"; Chloë, a Chr. female:—Chloe.

The Greek word *chlōrŏs* [Strong's 5515], from which we get "chlorophyll," appears four times in the New Testament. *Chloros* occurs once in the Gospel of Mark and three other times in the book of Revelation. It corresponds to the underlined words in the following passages.

When Jesus was about to feed a multitude, Mark says, "Then He commanded them to make them all sit down in groups on the green grass" (Mark 6:39). In Revelation 6:8, John used it with regard to the "pale" horse. In Revelation 8 it describes grass: "The first angel sounded: And hail and fire followed, mingled with blood, and they were thrown to the earth. And a third of the trees were burned up, and all green grass was burned up" (Rev. 8:7).

The final usage of *chloros* occurs within the context of the blowing of the fifth trumpet: "They [the angels] were commanded not to harm the grass of the earth, or any green thing, or any tree, but only those men who do not have the seal of God on their foreheads" (Rev. 9:4).

Of the four references to the word *chloros* in the New Testament, three clearly mean "green." In two out of the three instances in the book of Revelation it is translated "green." So, why would translators interpret the fourth horse of Revelation 6 as "pale"? It may be because the horse's rider is Death, which brings to mind a pale/green sickly color. However, like the other four horses, this horse comes from heaven. It carries its message from the throne room of God. It is true that many reject the gospel, but is the good news of salvation a sickly message or one of health? That the horse is green can bring to mind a picture of strength and health and can symbolize life and faith. The living green of our earth points to God as one who creates and sustains. Perhaps we have been too quick to assign the word "pale" to this horse, even if it's rider is called Death. What does the Bible say about death?

Death in the Bible

The Greek word for death used in Revelation 6:8 is *thanatos*. It occurs 119 times in the New Testament. *Vine's Expository Dictionary* makes the interesting statement that *thanatos* "is always, in Scripture, viewed as the penal consequence of sin" (*An Expository Dictionary of New Testament Words*, vol. 1, p. 276). Scripture pairs sin and death together like twins. Let us explore how these two words are linked.

While John does not use the word "sin" in Revelation, in his first letter he gives one of the clearest definitions of sin.

> Whoever commits sin also commits lawlessness, and sin is lawlessness. And you know that He was

> manifested to take away our sins, and in Him there is no sin. Whoever abides in Him does not sin. Whoever sins has neither seen Him nor known Him. Little children, let no one deceive you. He who practices righteousness is righteous, just as He is righteous. He who sins is of the devil, for the devil has sinned from the beginning. For this purpose the Son of God was manifested, that He might destroy the works of the devil. Whoever has been born of God does not sin, for His seed remains in him; and he cannot sin, because he has been born of God. In this the children of God and the children of the devil are manifest: Whoever does not practice righteousness is not of God, nor is he who does not love his brother. (1 John 3:4–10)

In these few words, John shines a light on several important points about sin. Sin is the transgression of the Law of God. If you continue in sin, you are part of the devil's family. Nevertheless, if you have been born again, you belong to the family of God. You have been given God's character. The Son of God was revealed to destroy the works of the devil (1 John 3:8), and the works of the devil are sinful. Yet, how is sin related to death?

The apostle Paul describes sin as acting in opposition to the law of God (see Rom. 7:7–12). In Romans 6:23 he relates sin to death. "The wages of sin is death (*thanatos*)" (Rom. 6:23). In other words, the result of sin is death. What then is death? It is the opposite of life. We know we are alive because we think and feel, we eat and sleep, we solve problems, and we make mistakes. In the end, there is death. When our hearts stop beating, the process of returning to the dust of the ground begins. Solomon explains death like this: "For the living know that they will die; but the dead know nothing, and they have no more reward, for the memory of them is forgotten" (Eccles. 9:5). It is an unpleasant fact that when you are dead, you are truly dead. Nobody is sort of dead.

Just what is the relationship between death and sin? Paul tells us: "Therefore, just as through one man sin [*hamartia*] entered the world, and death [*thanatos*] through sin, and thus death [*thanatos*] spread to all men, because all sinned [*hamartanō*]" (Rom. 5:12). Because of the sin of Adam, we are all destined to die and be buried on this earth. Sin causes death; it will cause your death.

Nevertheless, there is hope. Consider the conclusion of Paul's statement in Romans 6. "For the wages of sin is death, but the gift of God is eternal life in Christ Jesus our Lord" (Rom. 6:23). If the gospel message that comes from the throne of God is good news, then we may see that the rider of the green horse is intended to be a message that brings life to those who will receive it, but death to those who reject it. Eternal life comes to those who receive Christ. "For God so loved the world that He gave His only begotten Son, that whoever believes in Him should not perish but have everlasting life" (John 3:16).

So, if all the riders of Revelation 6 come from the throne of God with a message of salvation, why would the rider of the fourth horse be called Death? Ellen White gives us some insight on this. She speaks of Christ, the "Prince of Peace," as coming with a sword. Then she says: "He desired to show the effect his teaching would have on different minds. One portion of the human family would receive him; the other portion would take sides with Satan, and would oppose Christ and all his followers" (*Review and Hera*ld, January 16, 1900). Not all will receive the gospel. Many will reject it and, even more, will rise up in rebellion against it and hate it, and will persecute and destroy those who accept it and proclaim obedience to God's law.

In the end, they will see the One who brings life and salvation as the bearer of death and destruction. Do you remember what the leaders of Israel called Jesus? Ellen White reminds us:

> ... Though He was the Prince of Peace, His coming must be as the unsheathing of a sword. ... He who was the foundation of the ritual and economy of Israel would be looked upon as its enemy and destroyer. He who had proclaimed the law upon Sinai would be condemned as a transgressor. He who had come to break the power of Satan would be denounced as *Beelzebub*. (*The Desire of Ages*, p. 111, emphasis supplied)

It is amazing to think that the Prince of Peace was called an enemy and destroyer, that the Light Giver was called a transgressor, and that the One who destroys evil was called Beelzebub, the devil. When people choose to believe the lies of Satan and turn away from the gospel, their thinking becomes distorted. That which is white they call black, and that which is black they call white. How can truth be turned so upside down? The lies of Satan about Jesus become truth in the minds of those who oppose the message of God to the world. (See 2 Thes. 2:11, 12.)

Another way to say this is that God's message to the earth is life or death. The choice is ours. We learn through the symbolism of Revelation 6 and the fourth rider that there are those who will view this message as Death and Hell (which is "the grave"). Are the children of evil correct? Can the gospel of Jesus be called Death and the Grave? Let us look at this gospel message and discern why some will call it a message of death.

Death and Life

Jesus tells us in John 3:16 that we have a choice. We can choose to believe or not to believe. We can choose to "perish" or to "have everlasting life." If perishing is the opposite of having "everlasting life," then we are safe to say that *perish* means "everlasting death." Paul provides this contrast as well, when he writes: "For the wages of sin is death, but the gift of God is eternal life in Christ Jesus our Lord" (Rom. 6:23). If God's gift is *eternal* life, then can we not assume that the rejection of this gift is *eternal* death? If we do not believe in the Son, we will earn "everlasting death."

The theme of *choosing* runs all through Scripture. It began with the "first Adam" (1 Cor. 15:45) and continues down to each one of us. The message of the gospel of Jesus Christ is a message that demands a choice. We cannot avoid choosing. The final message that goes out to the world through the representation of the four horsemen of the Apocalypse is a message that either will be received or it will be rejected. It will bring life, or it will bring death. There is no riding the fence; there is no "in between"; it will bring a response.

What was mankind's first choice between life and death?

> Now the serpent was more cunning than any beast of the field which the Lord God had made. And he said to the woman, "Has God indeed said, 'You shall not eat of every tree of the garden'?" And the woman said to the serpent, "We may eat the fruit of the trees of the garden; but of the fruit of the tree which is in the midst of the garden, God has said, 'You shall not eat it, nor shall you touch it, lest you die.'" Then the serpent said to the woman, "You will not surely die....'" (Gen. 3:1-4)

Adam and Eve had a choice to make. God outlined it very clearly. Yet, they chose to believe the serpent and to sin against God. Consequently, death was introduced to all mankind. God wanted them to know that the "death" He warned them about was not a temporary state, but *eternal* death. Paul explains: "Therefore, just as through one man sin entered the world, and death through sin, and thus death spread to all men, because all sinned" (Rom. 5:12).

We must recognize that there is more than one use of "death" in Scripture. Moses brought the choice of life and death before Israel when renewing the covenant at Moab. It was a choice God put before the people before entering the Promised Land. He states, "See, I have set before you today life and good, death and evil ..." (Deut. 30:15). What did God mean by "life" and "death" in this passage? Ellen White explains:

> While life is the inheritance of the righteous, death is the portion of the wicked. Moses declared to Israel: "I have set before thee this day life and good, and death and evil." Deuteronomy 30:15. The death referred to in these scriptures is not that pronounced upon Adam, for all mankind suffer the penalty of his transgression. It is "the second death" that is placed in contrast with everlasting life. (*The Great Controversy*, p. 544)

When we die, we all go into the grave. Yet, the plan of salvation provides a way out. Though all mankind will be resurrected, the just are resurrected into everlasting life and the unjust are resurrected into damnation. The final judgment of God will place on the wicked the final penalty of transgression, which is the "second death." This "second death" is a death that will not end. There is no resurrection from the "second death."

Notice the contrast of life and death when we compare Romans 6:23 and Deuteronomy 30:15 in the following table:

Verses	King James Version	With added contrast
Rom. 6:23	For the wages of sin is death; but the gift of God is eternal life through Jesus Christ our Lord.	For the wages of sin is [the second] death; but the gift of God is eternal life through Jesus Christ our Lord.
Deut. 30:15	See, I have set before thee this day life and good, and death and evil;	See, I have set before thee this day [everlasting] life and good, and [the second] death and evil;

What is the "second death?" We have learned that it is not describing that which happens when the heart stops and the mind ceases to work. That death is the one that is, as we often hear, "as sure as taxes." This first death takes one to the grave, but it is not final. The "second death" is different. It is placed in contrast with "everlasting life." Obadiah tells us that the "second death" will be the separation that has no end. He says, "And they shall be as though they had never been" (Obad. 16).

Revelation speaks in several places about the second death. Jesus describes Himself in the first chapter: "I *am* He who lives, and was dead, and behold, I am alive forevermore. Amen. And I have the keys of Hades and of Death" (Rev. 1:18). Notice the contrast between "alive forevermore" and "dead." This death is the final punishment of the wicked.

There are references in Revelation to the actual phrase "second death" as well. For instance, when speaking to the church of Smyrna, Jesus says, "He who overcomes shall not be hurt by the second death" (Rev. 2:11). Overcomers will receive the crown of life and will not be touched by this final death. In speaking of the saints reigning with Christ for 1,000 years John writes, "Blessed and holy is he who has part in the first resurrection. Over such the second death has no power, but they shall be priests of God and of Christ, and shall reign with Him a thousand years" (Rev. 20:6). Just as there is a second death, the Bible also speaks of a second resurrection.

The first resurrection, which was mentioned above, is for the righteous. John writes in his Gospel about two resurrections: "Do not marvel at this; for the hour is coming in which all who are in the graves will hear His voice and come forth—those who have done good, to the resurrection of life, and those who have done evil, to the resurrection of condemnation" (John 5:28, 29). The second chance at life for those whom God raises at the second resurrection is only for judgment and the lake of fire. Notice how Revelation describes this punishment. "Then Death and Hades were cast into the lake of fire. This is the second death. And anyone not found written in the Book of Life was cast into the lake of fire" (Rev. 20:14).

The twin expression "Death and Hell" brings to mind our passage on the fourth horseman who rides the green horse. Death and Hell will be thrown into the lake of fire (Rev. 20:14). These personified entities represent the results of sin. They will be cast into the lake of fire and will undergo the second death. This lake of fire will consume them. Who are cast into this lake of fire besides Death and Hell? The passage says that it is "anyone not found written in the Book of Life." The wicked and the unjust are not written in the Book of Life. This second death in the lake of fire is the death that sinners will die. It will be a final separation of sin and sinners from the Creator.

Another passage lists in detail the types of people who will experience the second death. "But the cowardly, unbelieving, abominable, murderers, sexually immoral, sorcerers, idolaters, and all liars shall have their part in the lake which burns with fire and brimstone, which is the second death" (Rev. 21:8). The second death is a fact of life. It is reserved until God judges human beings according to their deeds. People who turn from the gospel actually die twice, the first time is before or at the second coming of Christ, the second will be after the final judgment.

Deuteronomy: Choosing Life or Death

When Moses set before the people a choice between life and death, he was offering them the gospel. When he said, "See, I have set before you today life and good, death and evil ... (Deut. 30:15) it was more than the first death he was speaking about. Ellen White links this same passage with Paul's statement, "For the wages of sin is death, but the gift of God is eternal life in Christ Jesus our Lord" (Rom. 6:23). She says, "The death referred to in these scriptures is not that pronounced upon Adam, for all mankind suffer the penalty of his transgression. It is the 'second death' that is placed in contrast with everlasting life" (*The Great Controversy*, p. 544). Both Paul and Moses set the gospel before mankind. It is a message of life or death, which demands a response. The fourth horse of Revelation 6 presents life or death.

There is one more interesting tie between Revelation 6 and Deuteronomy 28. Though separated by thousands of years in time, the correlation is startling. Just as God spoke to literal Israel before entering the Promised Land, so the Lord speaks to spiritual Israel as they enter the heavenly Canaan. What are the blessings that God promised His people? If they followed His instructions, He promised: "Blessed shall be the fruit of your body ... Blessed shall be your basket and your kneading bowl. Blessed shall you be when you come in, and blessed shall you be when you go out." (Deut. 28:4–6). There are also the blessings of protection from their enemies, blessings on their storehouses, blessings on their gardens, and more. In summary, God promised to bless their health, to supply them with abundant food, and to give them His protection.

The Lord also tells them what will happen if they do not choose to obey Him. "Cursed shall you be in the city, and cursed shall you be in the country. Cursed shall be your basket and your kneading bowl. Cursed shall be the fruit of your body and the produce of your land ..." (Deut. 28:16–18). He lists many more curses, but these can all be summarized under pestilence, sword, and famine.

Can anyone fail to see the contrast between the blessings and the curses of God?

The blessings of God, if you obey!	The curses of God, if you do not obey!
Health Protection Food	Pestilence Sword Famine

There is an amazing parallel to these curses in the message of the fourth horse in Revelation 6. Do you remember what it says? "And power was given to them over a fourth of the earth, to kill with sword, with hunger, with death ..." (Rev. 6:8). God's message to His people in the wilderness is the same message for people today. We choose blessings or curses, life or death. Judgment results from our choice. Jesus stated it like this: "... he who hears My word and believes in Him who sent Me has everlasting life, and shall not come into judgment, but has passed from death into life" (John 5:24).

The Wrath of God

Another way to understand "death" as brought on by the gospel—the widespread destruction that is symbolized by the fourth horseman—comes by looking at the concept of God's wrath against sin. We know the gospel brings life to those who accept it, but we discover in Scripture what happens to those who reject God's life-saving message. Notice Paul's classic statement about the power of the gospel and the wrath of God.

> For I am not ashamed of the gospel of Christ, for it is the power of God to salvation for everyone who believes, for the Jew first and also for the Greek. For in it the righteousness of God is revealed from faith to faith; as it is written, *"The just shall live by faith."* For the wrath of God is revealed from heaven against all ungodliness and unrighteousness of men, who suppress the truth in unrighteousness. (Rom. 1:16–18)

There are two paths from which to choose, according to Paul. If you believe in Jesus Christ and surrender your heart to Him, He justifies you, and gives you a new life. However, if you choose ungodliness, God's wrath will be revealed against your sin. Why must God's wrath be revealed? In speaking of the Jewish leaders and priests who persistently rejected light and stifled the convictions of the Holy Spirit, Ellen White explains,

> The wrath of God is not declared against unrepentant sinners merely because of the sins they have committed, but because, when called to repent, they choose to continue in resistance, repeating the sins of the past in defiance of the light given them. If the Jewish leaders had submitted to the convicting power of the Holy Spirit, they would have been pardoned; but they were determined not to yield. In the same way, the sinner, by continued resistance, places himself where the Holy Spirit cannot influence him. (*The Acts of the Apostles*, p. 62)

The penalty of sin is not directed to sinners merely because of the sins that they have committed, but because they refuse to turn back to God. When men turn down God's invitation, they must expect consequences. The wrath of God is coming. Notice how Ellen White describes what Jesus is doing in heaven during this time.

> I was taken off in vision to the most holy place, where I saw Jesus still interceding for Israel. On the bottom of His garment was a bell and a pomegranate, a bell and a pomegranate. Then I saw that Jesus would not leave the most holy place until every case was decided either for salvation or destruction, and that the wrath of God could not come until Jesus had finished His work in the most holy place, laid off His priestly attire, and clothed Himself with the garments of vengeance. Then Jesus will step out from between the Father and men, and God will keep silence no longer, but pour out His wrath on those who have rejected His truth ... then the seven last plagues will be poured out. (*Christian Experience and Teachings of Ellen G. White*, p. 100)

There is a principle of heaven that you need to know about. What you sow you will reap (Gal. 6:7). Nevertheless, the gospel of Jesus has opened the way of salvation for every human being.

> [Christ] died that sin might be made to appear exceeding sinful, the hateful thing that it is. By his death he became the possessor of the keys of hell and of death. Satan could no longer reign without a rival, and be reverenced as a god. Temples had been erected to him, and human sacrifices offered on his altars. But the emancipation papers of the race have

been signed by the blood of the Son of God. A way has been opened for the message of hope and mercy to be carried to the ends of the earth ... (*The Youth's Instructor*, June 28, 1900)

Jesus has opened the way for the rider of the green horse to give "the message of hope and mercy to be carried to the ends of the earth." Jesus has overcome. He has the keys of life, and He is sending a messenger to carry this good news to the world.

Summary

Just as Moses set before the people the choice of life and death, so God sets before people today the message of the gospel. Just as Moses pleaded for the people to "choose life" (Deut. 30:19), so God pleads with people to accept Christ. Each of the four horsemen of Revelation 6 carries a message to the ends of the earth to bring salvation to all people. Yet, for some, the message will be rejected. For those who turn away from the life-giving (green) message, the message turns into one of death (pale) and destruction. It is not God's purpose to bring death and destruction, but these result when men turn from the saving truth of Jesus. The consequence of sin is death. Thank God that the gift He offers through Jesus is life! Which will you choose?

Chapter 9

FOUR SOILS, FOUR RESPONSES

It is a beautiful spring day. You have just loaded your wheelbarrow with seeds and fertilizer. Your garden has been tilled and you begin to plant. You can already taste the mouthwatering fruits and vegetables that will soon come up. Since you will be gone for a few weeks, you set your automatic sprinkler to make sure the plants are watered well. When you come back home, you discover that hardly anything is growing. Most gardeners would start to investigate the problem. Was there enough water? Were there rodents or pests that ate the seeds? Did the plants get too much fertilizer? What happened? There is more to gardening than just planting seeds.

Having looked at the four horsemen of the Apocalypse and their messages, we will now consider a fascinating parable Jesus told to explain how the gospel is like seed that is scattered over different kinds of soil. Not all seed sewn bears fruit. This parable is a window to open our understanding of the four horsemen of Revelation 6 with even greater clarity as we ask: *What might four horsemen and four different types of soil have in common?*

The Parable of the Sower

> On the same day Jesus went out of the house and sat by the sea. And great multitudes were gathered together to Him, so that He got into a boat and sat; and the whole multitude stood on the shore. Then

> He spoke many things to them in parables, saying: "Behold, a sower went out to sow. And as he sowed, some seed fell by the wayside; and the birds came and devoured them. Some fell on stony places, where they did not have much earth; and they immediately sprang up because they had no depth of earth. But when the sun was up they were scorched, and because they had no root they withered away. And some fell among thorns, and the thorns sprang up and choked them. But others fell on good ground and yielded a crop: some a hundredfold, some sixty, some thirty. He who has ears to hear, let him hear!" (Matt. 13:1–9)

Jesus then gives the heavenly interpretation of the parable.

> Therefore hear the parable of the sower: When anyone hears the word of the kingdom, and does not understand it, then the wicked one comes and snatches away what was sown in his heart. This is he who received seed by the wayside. But he who received the seed on stony places, this is he who hears the word and immediately receives it with joy; yet he has no root in himself, but endures only for a while. For when tribulation or persecution arises because of the word, immediately he stumbles. Now he who received seed among the thorns is he who hears the word, and the cares of this world and the deceitfulness of riches choke the word, and he becomes unfruitful. But he who received seed on the good ground is he who hears the word and understands it, who indeed bears fruit and produces: some a hundredfold, some sixty, some thirty. (Matt. 13:18–23)

What is God teaching us through the sowing of seeds? Planting is not simply a matter of throwing seeds on the ground and then returning in a few months for the harvest. The parable teaches that a bountiful crop will occur if the seed is placed in good soil. Jesus is not teaching principles of farming; He is instructing us about the heart of man.

Let us look more carefully at the different parts of the Parable of the Sower. What is the seed that was sown? Jesus explains in Matthew 13:19 that it is "the word of the kingdom." In Matthew 4:23 Jesus went about casting this seed. There it is called "the gospel of the kingdom." Paul, in Romans 1:16, explains that the gospel of Christ is "the power of God to salvation." The power of Heaven is in the seed!

Yet, there is more to the parable than identifying the seed. Christ wants us to understand that not all seed sewn bears fruit. The harvest is dependent on the reaction of the soil on which the seed has fallen. There is a cause-and-effect link between the growth of the seed and the type of soil into which the seed has fallen. One thing makes the other thing happen. This relationship can be seen with a simple example. If we eat too much fatty food, we can get heart disease. That is to say, that eating too much fatty food is the *cause* and heart disease is the *effect*.

What is the *one thing* that makes *the other thing* happen in the Parable of the Sower? We know that the heavenly seed does not change. So, what causes the seed to grow into a mature plant that produces fruit? It is the character of the soil. It is the type of soil that the seed falls into that determines whether the seed will grow into a plant that produces fruit. In other words, the type of soil into which the seed is sown—the *cause*—determines if the seed will grow into a mature plant with fruit—the *effect*.

Jesus tells us that there are four ways the seed is received or rejected by the soil. In three of those soils (the hard soil, the stony soil, and the soil overrun by weeds) we are told that the seed stops growing and is destroyed. In the fourth soil, the good soil, the seed grows into a mature plant and produces a bountiful harvest. The spiritual message from the Master Sower is clear: the gospel seed will not be well received by everyone; the bountiful harvest will be seen in only some hearts.

The Wayside Soil

So, what happens to the gospel seed in men who have hearts like the wayside? Matthew 13:4 says, "... the birds came and *devoured them*." The wayside is a well-beaten path, hardened by the feet of hundreds of travelers. Birds will eat the seed that falls on such a path. There is no harvest from such soil.

What hardens hearts so that the gospel message does not penetrate? Our hearts become hard when we indulge in sinful actions. Lives of selfish focus make us resistant to the message of the gospel. Such hearts are so hard that they do not even feel troubled when they hear the good news. Christ's invitation does not move them. His warnings about the consequences of rejecting His invitation do not bother them. Those who have chosen this path of life are here for the pleasures of today, and they are not concerned about tomorrow.

The Stony Soil

What happened to the gospel seed that fell in the stony soil? Jesus says, "Some fell upon stony places, where they had not much earth: and they immediately sprang up because they had no depth of earth: but when the sun was up they were scorched, and because they had no root *they withered away*" (Matt. 13:5, 6).

The stony-ground soil appears good on the surface, but hidden in this ground are large stones, which inhibit the growth of the plant because its roots cannot dig deep in the soil to find enough nutrients and water to sustain its life when the heat comes. Stones symbolize a hardened selfish heart. These hearers trust in their own works. They believe that their own character and their own goodness will save them. When the hot summer sun—the fiery test of temptation—comes to young plants of the gospel in such soil, they wither, because the stones of selfishness have blocked the roots of trust in Christ. Spiritual plants cannot survive the heat, without the water of life. If these stones of selfishness are not removed, they will be the cause of our death. We cannot keep both the joy of the gospel and the stones of selfishness in our hearts.

Soil with Weeds

What happened to the gospel seed that fell on the soil that is filled with thorns and weeds? "And some fell among thorns, and the thorns sprung up and *choked them*" (Matt. 13:7). This soil also allows the seed to grow at first, but the weeds of wealth and pride and pleasure soon choke and kill the message of the gospel.

> The destructive nature of weeds is a reality that Ellen White warns us of: "The gospel seed often falls among thorns and noxious weeds; and *if* there is not a moral transformation in the human heart, *if* old habits and practices and the former life of sin are not left behind, *if* the attributes of Satan are not expelled from the soul, the wheat crop will be choked. The thorns will come to be the crop, and will kill out the wheat" (*Christ's Object Lessons*, p. 50, *emphasis added*).

Good Soil

Let us look at the last soil. What effect did the gospel seed have in the good soil? The Bible tells what the seed that fell on the good ground represents: "But he who received seed on the good ground is he who hears the word and understands *it*, who indeed *bears fruit and produces*: some a hundredfold, some sixty, some thirty" (Matt. 13:23). The good soil is soft and receptive to receiving the seed. It is void of rocks and weeds. The seed grows into a mature plant and then it bears fruit. It is a perfect description of a repentant heart.

This good soil represents those who have heard the words of Jesus and have allowed these words to break their hearts. They are repentant, and they turn from sin, and, with His help, have the stones of selfishness and the weeds of worldly influences removed. They realize that cultivation of the heart happens at the feet of Jesus every day. In time these people will want to stand next to the Master Sower and cast the seed of the gospel themselves to watch the power of the word of God produce a large harvest.

Jesus wants to save lost human beings. He is the Sower. That is why He is seen broadcasting the seed. He came to this earth to give the gospel invitation to you. The seed from Heaven, if allowed to grow in your heart, will produce life in you. Jesus tells us that it will produce fruit in your life—fruit that will be given to others and produce life in them. This is the principle of the seed from Heaven. Life from God produces life.

The End Result

What other lesson is God teaching us? We have been taught how the heart of man responds to the gospel invitation of Jesus Christ. We know what happens. We have studied how the reactions of hearts are like the wayside, the stony ground, the ground covered with weeds and thorns, and the good ground. Did you notice that only one in four chooses to turn back to Him? If only one heart receives the blessing of God, what happens to those who choose not to accept the invitation?

We need to draw attention to something that the parable mentioned but did not emphasize. What was the reaction to the seed for each soil? We will place each reaction in a table to help us visualize this important principle.

The Soils	The Reactions of the Seed in the Soil
Seed on the pathway	The seed was eaten by birds—death.
Seed in the stony ground	The young plants were destroyed by heat—death.
Seed in the thorny ground	The growing plants were destroyed by choking—death.
Seed in the good ground	The mature plants yield a bountiful harvest—life!

The physical lesson of seed planted in different soils teaches us that the good ground produced life, while the other soils did not. Yet, it is the *spiritual lesson* we must not miss. The Bible tells us that accepting the gospel seed into the life results in eternal life. "For God so loved the world, that he gave his only begotten Son, that whosoever believeth in him should not perish, but have everlasting life" (John 3:16). This is the bountiful harvest we can expect. Believing on the Lord Jesus Christ results in life eternal, like the seed that fell in the good soil. However, rejecting the gospel seed results in loss—eternal loss. If you do not believe on Christ, you will *perish* like the seed that was eaten, like the young plants that withered, or like the plants that were choked by thorns.

Our reception of the gospel is a choice with eternal results. This same choice of life or death is seen in Romans 6:23. "For the wages of sin is *death*; but the gift of God is *eternal life* through Jesus Christ our Lord" (Rom. 6:23). This verse is Paul's version of the gospel invitation. It also gives the listener a choice. If you choose Jesus Christ, you will be given the gift of eternal life. If you do not choose Jesus Christ, and you continue in sin, you will receive death.

Life or Death

We know that in the Parable of the Sower there are four soils. These represent four reactions of the heart of man to the gospel invitation. Let us categorize the results of each of their choices, using the life or death formula. The wayside heart chooses death. The heart with the stones chooses death. The heart with the weeds and thorns chooses death. The good soil heart chooses life.

The gospel given by the sower	How the gospel is received	Life or death
Seed on the pathway	Eaten by birds	Everlasting death
Seed on the stony ground	Destroyed by heat	Everlasting death
Seed on the thorny ground	Destroyed by choking	Everlasting death
Seed on the good ground	Yields fruit of the Spirit	Eternal life

The spiritual lesson of the Parable of the Sower is clear. We are not dealing with the growth of seed in the soils, but with the eternal results of the gospel invitation to every heart.

The parable asks: How will you react to the invitation of the gospel? Will you ignore the invitation and go on with your pleasurable pursuits? Will you allow the gospel to reveal stones of selfishness or weeds of worldliness in your heart that you might be ignoring? How will you respond to this message from God? This parable is not asking you to examine your gardening practices. It is asking you to examine your heart. The question to each one should be: *Have I truly accepted the gospel and salvation? Or have I rejected God's message to me and will be lost?*

Ellen White writes: "The question of greatest importance to you is, How do you treat My message? Upon your reception or rejection of it your eternal destiny depends" (*Christ's Object Lessons*, p. 43). Do you believe those words? "How do you treat My message?" That *is* the question. The Master Sower, Jesus, has cast onto your heart a message of love and salvation. How will you respond?

Chapter 10

PARALLEL PICTURES: SEEDS AND HORSES

So, how do seeds and horses relate to one another? What do the Parable of the Sower and the four horsemen of the Apocalypse have in common? Are there parallels to these two Bible illustrations that increase our understanding of the book of Revelation? There may be more than you realize.

We have just studied about the message of the riders and found it very similar to the message of the Sower. Both the riders and the Sower carry the gospel invitation. Yet, the four horsemen have an additional work, a burden regarding the prophecies of Jesus in Revelation. It is important that we notice how people respond to the gospel, as we did in the Parable of the Sower. How is God's message, sent out from the throne room of heaven, received? Our eternal destiny hangs on this question. Their responses are either for life or for death.

Reactions of the Four Horseman

Let us consider the responses of the four horsemen. We have highlighted this passage to help us see these important responses.

> Now I saw when the Lamb opened one of the seals; and I heard one of the four living creatures saying with a voice like thunder, "Come and see." And I looked, and behold, a white horse. He who sat on

> it had a bow; and a crown was given to him: and he went out conquering and to conquer. When He opened the second seal, I heard the second living creature saying, "Come and see." Another horse, fiery red, went out. And it was granted to that the one who sat on it to take peace from the earth, and that *people* should kill one another; and there was given to him a great sword. When He opened the third seal, I heard the third living creature say, "Come and see." So I looked, and behold, a black horse, and he who sat on it had a pair of scales in his hand.... When He had opened the fourth seal, I heard the voice of the fourth living creature saying, "Come and see." So I looked, and behold, a pale horse. And the name of him who sat on it was Death, and Hades followed with him. And power was given to them over a fourth of the earth, to kill with sword, with hunger, with death, and by the beasts of the earth. (Rev. 6:1–5, 7, 8)

Can you begin to see the parallels with the Parable of the Sower? The reactions to the gospel are similar. The four horsemen all carry the gospel and the prophecies of Jesus Christ, yet their different features show they represent four different reactions. The message from the white horse rider produces life, but the messages from the riders on the red, black, and pale ("green") horses produce death.

The Parable of the Sower shows four responses to the gospel, and the four horsemen of the Apocalypse show four different reactions to the gospel. Notice the parallels.

The Gospel Carrier	The Reaction to the Gospel	"Life" or "Death"	Parable of the Sower
White horse rider	A Bow, a Crown, and Conquering The Righteousness of Christ	Accepting the gospel of Jesus Christ gives victory over sin	Good soil – abundant harvest
Red horse rider	Peace Removed, Men Kill One Another Peace vs. Fear	Rejecting the gospel of Jesus Christ result in the "second death"	Hard soil – birds eat the seed
Black horse rider	A Yoke, Making a Choice Freedom vs. Slavery	Rejecting the gospel of Jesus Christ result in the "second death"	Stony soil – plants wither in hot sun, no root
Green horse rider	War, Famine, Pestilence, and Beasts Life vs. Death	Rejecting the gospel of Jesus Christ result in the "second death"	Soil with thorns – weeds grow up and choke plants

Who Are the Horsemen?

The Parable of the Sower was God's way of teaching us how the hearts of men and women react to the gospel message of Jesus Christ. One heart accepts the gospel, while three hearts turn from it and from the Savior. It is a startling revelation that not every heart turns to God to be saved. This same theme is seen in the reaction to the messages of the four riders in Revelation 6.

Each rider is sent from the throne of God, and each rider carries the gospel and the prophecies of Jesus Christ in Revelation. The riders have God's command to carry His message to the end of the world. They are carried to their destinations by the variously colored horses of heaven. God wants you to know that His people are His messengers. It is He who sends them out with the last message of hope for the world. It is *you* who are the rider on God's apocalyptic warhorse, carrying God's final message to the world. He gives advance warning that the response of most people to this precious message will not be positive. Ellen White reminds us of our duty to carry the light of truth:

> The book of Revelation must be opened to the people. Many have been taught that it is a sealed book, but it is sealed to those only who reject truth and light. The truths that it contains must be proclaimed, that people may have an opportunity to prepare for the events which are so soon to take place. The Third Angel's Message must be presented as the only hope for the salvation of a perishing world.
>
> The perils of the last days are upon us, and in our work we are to warn the people of the danger they are in. Let not the solemn scenes that prophecy has revealed are soon to take place be left untouched. We are God's messengers, and we have no time to lose. Those who would be co-workers with our Lord Jesus Christ will show a deep interest in the truths found in this book. With pen and voice they will strive to make plain the wonderful things that Christ came from heaven to reveal. (*Signs of the Times*, July 4, 1906)

Based on what we learned from the Parable of the Sower and the four horsemen of the Apocalypse, we know a message will be carried to the world by the riders on the four horses sent from the throne of God. We have learned that these messages include the gospel of Jesus Christ and the Prophecies of Jesus Christ in Revelation. Revelation describes these as the Three Angel's Messages. These last messages are the "only hope for the salvation of a perishing world." It is our work to "warn the people of the danger they are in." Jesus is asking you today: *Will you answer the call? Will you prepare yourself physically, mentally, and spiritually to carry His message to the ends of the earth?*

Summary

Jesus' story of the farmer scattering seed demonstrates that not all seed is received in the same way. He teaches that a good harvest of grain can only come by plowing the hard earth, by removing the heavy stones, and by weeding out the thorns and thistles. It is not a lesson in farming; it is a message about salvation. The final consequences of how we receive the seed have eternal implications.

In a similar way, the four horsemen of Revelation 6 carry a message to the world. Like the scattered seed, they spread in all directions from the throne of God. Revelation discloses a prophetic emphasis to the gospel—Jesus is coming soon. The prophecies of Revelation show that the message is to be earnestly delivered, for we live in the time of the end. Not everyone will receive the message. Not all responses will be the same.

Reflecting on the Parable of the Sower, Ellen White writes:

> Christ represents the different results of the sowing as depending upon the soil. In every case the sower and the seed are the same. Thus He teaches that if the word of God fails of accomplishing its work

in our hearts and lives, the reason is to be found in ourselves. But the result is not beyond our control. True, we cannot change ourselves; but the power of choice is ours, and it rests with us to determine what we will become. (*Christ's Object Lessons*, p. 56)

When you are asked to present the gospel of Jesus Christ and the three angel's messages, you must be ready spiritually, mentally and physically. When you begin to give the message, you must allow the Spirit of God to woo the sinner, for the response to the message is not in your hands. The most disappointing response for you will be when people turn away from the light of God. But seed sowers trust God and sew anyway. The seed will do its work, if you do your part. God's harvest will come. Will you faithfully do your part in spreading the gospel?

Chapter 11

How Will You Respond?

In 2011, there were about 2,000 train/automobile collisions in the United States (Federal Railroad Administration Office of Safety Analysis, 2011 statistics). The year before, such collisions resulted in 261 deaths and over 810 serious injuries. Several factors contributed to these accidents, such as drowsy train operators and defective tracks. Interestingly enough, about fifty percent of vehicle-train collisions occurred at crossings with active warning devices, such as gates, lights, and bells. Drivers either ignored the warnings or they did not pay attention–and it cost many people their lives.

As we reflect back on the messages of the four horsemen of Revelation 6, we might think of them as giving a warning to the world. Signs point to the soon coming of Jesus. The Lord has not left us to wonder about the end of the age. The book of Revelation provides us with knowledge about things to come. When Jesus taught, more than once He said, "He who has ears to hear, let him hear!" (Matt. 11:15). Are you hearing the message of the four horsemen? In this chapter, we will consider what God is seeking to communicate to us personally.

Warning the World

When we began our study of Revelation 4, we entered the throne room of heaven. God the Father and Jesus Christ were seated in the center of the heavenly sanctuary in accordance with the model of the earthly tabernacle. They were surrounded by special angels who sent out the four horses with their riders. The riders are the servants of God bearing a message for the world. When we place them in the diagram we have been building, what do we see?

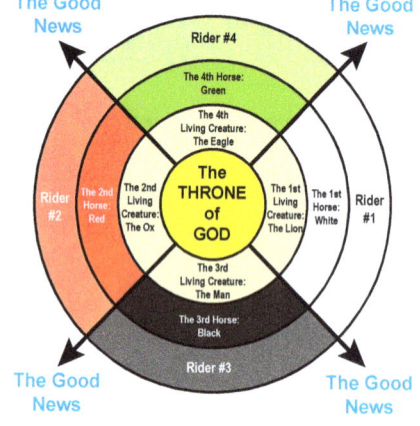

The diagram shows the movement of the messages that God sends out, beginning at His throne and spreading in every direction. According to the diagram, who is He trying to reach? It shows the channels God uses to communicate to men through His family.

God communicates His message of salvation through His angelic and human children. Revelation 4–6 illustrates the pattern of communication. A summary of what the message includes is found in Revelation 1, where John describes being on the Isle of Patmos "for the word of God and for the testimony of Jesus Christ" (Rev. 1:9). The "word of God" is the message of salvation. It is the gospel—the good news—about how God offers us a way out of sin and death into eternal life. The "testimony of Jesus Christ" concerns the prophecies of the Bible, including the book of Revelation (see Rev. 19:10).

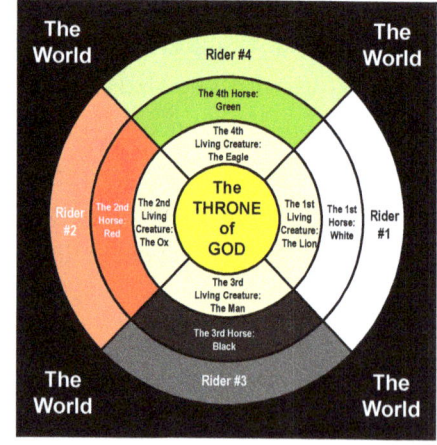

The four horsemen of the Apocalypse have the

same burden of spreading a message from God to the world. Like John, they are compelled to carry the good news and the prophecies of Jesus Christ. The message is the same, but the response to the message is different for each rider. As we learned in the Parable of the Sower, not all seed falls on good soil. Not all hearts receive the message. When sin is in the heart, the response to the gospel is different. So it is with the four horsemen leave the throne of God with the same message of salvation, it is received in different ways. The people of the earth will either receive the good news with victory and power, as portrayed by the white horse; or they will reject the message and live in fear, as portrayed by the red horse, in slavery, as portrayed by the black horse, and ultimately they will die, as portrayed by the green horse.

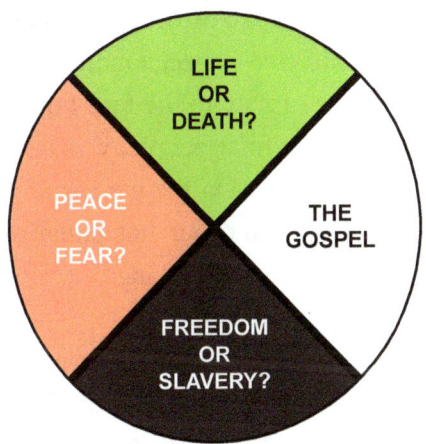

God did not give John a written manuscript. Neither did He give him a scroll or a document concerning things that are going to happen before the end of time. The Lord "showed" John "things which must shortly take place" (Rev. 1:1). He was given a vision that he might see and understand God's will. The Lord wants to do the same thing for each of us. He wants us to "see" how heaven is focused on saving man. He also wants us to know the future of this world. If the basic messages of the four riders were depicted as a warning sign, they could be represented somewhat like a railroad crossing sign. The messages of the four horses are a warning from the throne of God to be carried to the ends of the earth. They lay out the choice that is placed before every human being.

The Three Angel's Messages and the Four Riders

We have spent much time studying the four horses of Revelation 6. We know they are sent out from the throne room of God. We discovered that they go out to all four corners of the earth. They carry a message of salvation and warning to the world. The message is not received in the same way by all.

As we have learned something by comparing one part of Scripture with another, we must ask: Is there a more specific explanation of this end-time message in the book of Revelation? Yes, it is found in Revelation 14 and called the three angels' messages. If God's end-time remnant are to give a special message of warning to the world, do these messages relate to the four horsemen? John, as a representative of God's final people, was told, "You must prophesy again ..." (Rev. 10:11). Do the messages of the three angels have any correlation to the four horsemen of Revelation 6? They do. The messages of the three angels follow the pattern of the messages of the four horsemen.

In Revelation 6, John sees a *white* horse and its rider going east with a message. The symbol of a crown and the words "conquering" indicate victory. The message of this horse is accepted. Men and women are filled with the victory of salvation in Jesus Christ. There is a similarity in the first part of the first angel's message of Revelation 14. Notice what it says. "Then I saw another angel flying in the midst of heaven, having the everlasting gospel to preach to those who dwell on the earth—to every nation, tribe, tongue, and people" (Rev. 14:6). Here is a message that is going out "conquering and to conquer." It is received by some. A crown will be given to those who accept it. The other horses represent the results of the gospel's rejection.

Back to Revelation 6, John next sees a *red* horse and its rider going west with a message. The reaction of people to the message is depicted as peace being taken from the earth. In other words, *fear* results in death and the sword. This fear comes from rejecting the gospel. When we look at the second part of the first angel's message, we read these words: "Fear God and give glory to Him, for the hour of His judgment has come ..." (Rev. 14:7). When accepted, the judgment hour message causes people to worship God in awe and respect; when it is rejected, people respond to the judgment with great fear and trembling. Christ came to bring peace, but, those who reject His peace respond in fear and "kill one another" (Rev. 6:4).

Returning to Revelation 6, John then sees a rider on a *black* horse, raising a symbol of a yoke. A call is being made to make a choice. Will people be yoked to Christ or Satan? Will listeners chose to cooperate with Christ and carry a "light burden," or will they follow the devil and become slaves under an iron yoke? What power will rule the life? Notice how the second angel's message relates to this choice. "And another angel followed, saying, 'Babylon is fallen, is fallen, that great city, because she has made all nations drink of the wine of the wrath of her fornication" (Rev. 14:8). The wine of Babylon symbolizes the false teachings of a false church. Babylon seeks to force people to follow her deceptions. They must choose whether they will be connected to Christ or whether they will be enslaved to Babylon.

Finally, John sees, in Revelation 6, a *green* horse whose rider is Death, with Hades as his companion. Death and Hades are given authority to kill with the sword and to bring hunger and pestilence to the earth. Even though this "green" horse could symbolize life and hope, it turns into a message of death for those who reject the gospel. The prophetic message of the third angel is profound—"If anyone worships the beast

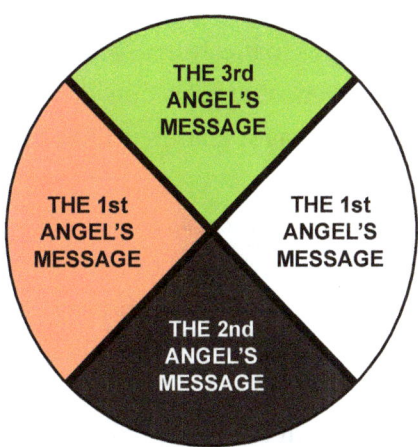

and his image, and receives *his* mark on his forehead or on his hand, he himself shall also drink of the wine of the wrath of God, which is poured out full strength into the cup of His indignation. He shall be tormented with fire and brimstone in the presence of the holy angels and in the presence of the Lamb" (Rev. 14:9, 10). The destruction here described is the second death explained in Revelation 20. It is the final eradication of all sin and sinners from the universe. It is a separation from God and the source of all life, which comes from the throne room of heaven.

Jesus is coming again. The Lord desires to save every one of His children. The coming of Christ is a blessed event all should anticipate. However, unless we are ready, it is a fearful time. God gave prophetic messages throughout history to warn His people to turn to Him. The prophetic messages of the three angels also warn us that those who turn away from God will fear the coming judgment because they have chosen the doctrines of Babylon, which are opposed to the law of God. Because people have chosen to follow the beast and turn from God, they will be placed in the group marked for eternal death.

Revelation chapters 4 through 6 show us how God is working to save the world. The Lord works through angels to communicate warnings to His servants, who then take those warnings to the world. Like riders on horses, the message is to go out to every corner of our planet. God calls each of us to receive the gospel and become like Paul Revere, warning others of approaching destruction. Revelation 14 describes these messages and their reception or rejection in greater detail.

The message of Revelation is simple: *Get ready!* The gospel message is the same for all ages. From the writings of Moses and Daniel to the words of Christ, we are presented with a choice. Our preparation for the soon coming of Jesus is to choose life. We learn from the Parable of the Sower and from the four horsemen of the Apocalypse that not everyone will choose to follow God.

Some will follow Babylon, worship the beast and receive its mark. Their choice will result in fear, slavery, and eventually the second death.

The opening of the seals in Revelation 6 shows God's work on our planet. It is God's desire to save us. He sends His messengers into all the earth. The message they bear invites men to turn and live. Turning to God and accepting the gospel means believing in truth and living by its light. Rejecting God means turning away from truth and believing the lies of Satan. Many will be deceived. That three of the soils in Jesus' parable did not receive the seed of truth shows how many will lose their salvation. That three of the four horsemen bear messages that represent death indicates that many will reject God's entreaties. Satan's deceptions appeal to the carnal nature. He causes people to believe that living for selfish pursuits will bring happiness, when Jesus taught that the cares of this world can choke and destroy our lives.

Believing a Lie

The deceiver of mankind began his evil work by leading Adam and Eve to believe a lie. He will use the same strategy until the end of time. We are confronted with the same question: *Will we believe the word of God or the lies of Satan?* Remember how Eve said to the serpent, "We may eat the fruit of the trees of the garden; but of the fruit of the tree which is in the midst of the garden, God has said, 'You shall not eat it, nor shall you touch it, lest you die'" (Gen. 3:2, 3). Eve knew the truth and was able to state it quickly and accurately. However, the serpent countered with a fabrication. His answer was slow, deliberate, and cunning. "You will not surely die. For God knows that in the day you eat of it your eyes will be opened, and you will be like God, knowing good and evil" (Gen. 3:4, 5). It was a lie and in direct contradiction to God's words.

Eve (and later Adam) chose to believe a lie. She did not live "by every word that proceeds from the mouth of God" (Matt. 4:4). Why did she think that God was trying to deceive her and keep her from becoming a god like Him? We do not know, but what we do know is that she chose to follow the path of the Devil. She ate the fruit. Then she became an agent of Satan and seduced her husband into taking the same step. Moments later, when she realized that she was naked and her conscience pricked her soul, Eve also realized that she had sinned. She was lost.

Yet, God was ready. Via the sacrificial system, God showed Adam and Eve the path back to Him. Eve confessed her sin, offered the sacrifice of a lamb, and was born again. God can be trusted. The Lord does not lie. His word is sure. It is "the substance of things hoped for, the evidence of things not seen" (Heb. 11:1). The truth of God is man's solution to the slavery of sin.

God's plan of salvation leads us out of confusion and lies and back into truth. This message is not only to be received into the heart but also taken to the entire world. Like John, we too must live "for the word of God and for the testimony of Jesus Christ" (Rev. 1:9). Are you a disciple of Jesus on this island called planet Earth? Are you ready to take the last message of warning found in Daniel and Revelation, and like a rider on horseback carry it to the ends of the world? Jesus told John to *write* about the things he was shown. Today Christ calls us to *proclaim* these things. Will you join God's horsemen in proclaiming the message?

We invite you to view the complete
selection of titles we publish at:

www.TEACHServices.com

Scan with your mobile
device to go directly
to our website.

Please write or email us your praises, reactions, or
thoughts about this or any other book we publish at:

P.O. Box 954
Ringgold, GA 30736

info@TEACHServices.com

TEACH Services, Inc., titles may be purchased in bulk for
educational, business, fund-raising, or sales promotional use.
For information, please e-mail:

BulkSales@TEACHServices.com

Finally, if you are interested in seeing
your own book in print, please contact us at

publishing@TEACHServices.com

We would be happy to review your manuscript for free.

www.ingramcontent.com/pod-product-compliance
Lightning Source LLC
Chambersburg PA
CBHW070556160426
43199CB00014B/2521